W9-CLA-634

Getting in TTouch
with
Your Cat

BY THE SAME AUTHOR

The Tellington TTouch: *A Breakthrough Technique to Train and Care for Your Favorite Animal*

Getting in TTouch: *Understand and Influence Your Horse's Personality*

Let's Ride with Linda Tellington-Jones: *Fun and TTeamwork with Your Horse or Pony*

Improve Your Horse's Well-Being: *A Step-by-Step Guide to TTouch and TTeam Training*

Getting in TTouch with Your Dog: *A Gentle Approach to Influencing Behavior, Health, and Performance*

Getting in TTouch with Your Cat

A New and Gentle Way to Harmony, Behavior, and Well-Being

LINDA TELLINGTON-JONES
Translation by Sybil Taylor

TRAFALGAR SQUARE PUBLISHING
North Pomfret, Vermont

First Published in the United States of America in 2003 by
Trafalgar Square Publishing
North Pomfret, Vermont 05053

Printed in Hong Kong

Originally published in the German language as *TTouch® für Katzen*
by Franckh-Kosmos Verlags-GmbH & Co., Stuttgart, 2003

Library of Congress Control Number: 2003107947

ISBN 1-57076-254-6

Cover design by Carrie Fradkin
Book layout by Molly Allen

Photographs by Gabriele Metz, Mulheim
Illustrations on pp. 62, 64, 67, 74 by Jeanne Kloepfer, Heidelberg
Illustrations on pp. 57, 70, 72, 80, 85, 87, 89 by Cornelia Koller, Schierhorn

10   9   8   7   6   5   4   3   2   1

DEDICATION

I dedicate this book to my sister Robyn Hood for all the years of friendship, collaboration, and support. There are not sufficient words to describe my love and appreciation. With immeasurable energy, she has accompanied me on the journey to develop TTouch and TTEAM. For twenty years, she has published the TTEAM newsletter, led the North American TTEAM Guild, and the Canadian TTEAM office, while spreading news of the work around the rest of the world.

Tellington TTouch for Cats

Cats and TTouch 1
Cats as Companions 5
TTouch for the Whole Family 6
Cats and Children 7
A Kitten Moves In 9
Stress-Free Travel 10
The First Hours in a New Home 11
Health and Well-Being 12
Unaltered Male Cats 13
The Breeding Visit 15
Mothers and Kittens 16
Stars of the Show 18
Adopting Animal-Shelter Cats 21
TTouch in the Animal Shelter 22
TTouch in Veterinary Practice 23
When a Cat Reaches the
    Senior Years 28
The Last Good-bye 29

Here We Go with TTouch

First Contact 33
Stay Right Here! 35
TTouches with Sheepskin 39
Grooming Your Cat's Fur 40
Gloves 42
Strong Cats 44

TTouches with a Feather 45
So You Don't Want to Come Out? 46
The Wicker Basket 51
Claw Trimming 52
Sensitive Cats 55

How and Why: Circle TTouches

A New Method 57
Abalone TTouch 62
Lying Leopard TTouch 64
Clouded Leopard TTouch 67
Llama TTouch 71
Chimp TTouch 72
Raccoon TTouch 74
Tiger TTouch 77

How and Why: Stroking TTouches

Noah's March 80
Python TTouch 82
Combination TTouch 83

Lick of the Cow's Tongue 85
Tarantula TTouch 87
Earthworm TTouch 89
Hair Slides 90

**How and Why:
Specific TTouches**

Ear TTouch 94
Mouth TTouch 98
Belly Lift 101
TTouch Circling on
   the Front Legs 104

TTouch Circling on the Hind
   Legs 106
TTouch on the Paws 108
Tail TTouch 109

TTouch Resources

TTouch Plan for Your Cat 111
Glossary 112
TTouch Resources 114
Acknowledgments 117
Index 118

TTouch for Cats

Knowledge of the Tellington TTouch, and how to use it, will open the door to a magical relationship with your cat. TTouch is like a secret, nonverbal language: a language that your cat will immediately understand, whether he or she is a wonderful, easy-to-care-for house cat, a capricious queen, or an aggressive "tiger!"

Cats and TTouch

A common belief holds that it's not possible for humans to affect the behavior of cats and that, in fact, it's far more likely that cats are the ones who change our behavior. Another widely held idea is that it's impossible to influence feline behavior once a cat is full grown.

In my experience, I have found the reverse to be true. I've seen shy, aggressive, anxious, and introverted cats totally alter their basic behavior after experiencing the TTouch. Actually, the TTouch affects more than behavior alone: It also improves the health and well-being of cats, promotes the

Through TTouch, you develop a particularly tender and intense relationship with your cat.

By using TTouch you can elicit lasting and positive behavior changes, as well as increase the well-being of your cat. And, if you do regular TTouch work, you too, will feel healthier. The pleasant benefits of TTouch are good for humans and animals alike.

healing process, supports animals during recovery from injury, illness, and surgery, and strengthens them in their senior years.

What is the Tellington TTouch?

The Tellington TTouch method—referred to as T-Touch—consists of gentle, connected, circular touches, and lifting and stroking movements on the skin. These touches alter behavior, improve well-being, and influence the relationship between cats and their humans. The TTouches can be done all over the cat's body. The goal of the TTouch is to stimulate cellular function and to awaken the innate "intelligence" within cells themselves. The list of animals helped is long—cats,

dogs, horses, orangutans, hamsters, elephants, whales, llamas, chimpanzees, and of course, humans, too.

With only a few minutes of TTouch each day, not only can you change your cat's personality and behavior, but you can also improve your own health and well-being at the same time by enjoying this unusual communication with your four-legged friend.

I first thought of using the TTouch with cats in 1984, during a one-week seminar for horse owners in Boulder, Colorado. One of the participants, a veterinarian's assistant, told us about a six-week-old kitten who had been brought to the clinic with a cold and little chance of survival.

In the evening, when the assistant was getting ready to

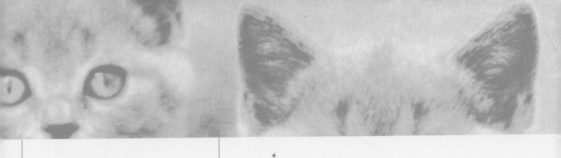

return to the vet clinic, I recommended that she try very tiny TTouches (the kind that today we call *Raccoon TTouches*) on the kitten and monitor the reaction. To her great surprise, during the night, the kitten's condition improved remarkably. At this point, it became clear that TTouch could dramatically affect the healing process.

▶ Like Jekyll and Hyde

In my life, I've been gifted with a number of wonderful cat companions, but one of them, a long-legged, slim, black feline with white chest markings, four white paws, white whiskers and a pair of radiant eyes, had the soul of a lioness in the body of a cat. I discovered her in an animal shelter in Clinton, New York, where I was conducting a three-day-long seminar, "TTouch for Companion Animals."

As I walked through the shelter's section that housed cats, a seemingly friendly kitten immediately ran up to the bars of the cage and began rubbing against them to attract my attention. However, when I reached out my hand, the cat struck out at me with bared claws.

The shelter's director suggested that this was the perfect animal for demonstrating our work.

We brought the kitten to the seminar room in a carrier, carefully opened it, and after first wrapping the cat in a towel, we began to work on her (see page 22). For the first session, I didn't work on her longer than ten minutes because she hissed each time I touched her and even tried to strike at me through the towel. The moment I took away the towel and gave her a chance to look at me, she became a friendly little kitten once again. None of us had ever seen such strange behavior in a cat. I suspected that she wanted to have contact, but at the same time, had no control over her aggressive reactions.

On the third day, as we gathered in the seminar room once again, I was certain that the kitten would continue her aggressive behavior, but, when I opened the carrier, she emerged all on her own and rubbed against me. We were all utterly amazed. "Would anyone like to adopt this cute kitten?" I asked. Everyone laughed, remembering her earlier behavior. At that moment, I knew that I would be the one to rescue her, and I felt my eyes well up with sudden tears of joy. This "hopeless" kitten had given up her "Jekyll and Hyde" mentality and conquered my heart.

The TTouch That Teaches

The TTouch method goes beyond a simple massage. The various TTouches are not only relaxing, but, it seems, they also activate intelligence—animals that are TTouched adapt with measurably more ease to unfamiliar surroundings and situations. This characteristic is especially important for a cat that is being introduced to a new home, an unfamiliar person or animal, or is experiencing the stresses of being at a cat show or at the vet.

The TTouches strengthen confidence and teach animals to think rather than to react.

One of the wonderful things about the various circling movements is that you don't have to use them in any specific order to be successful. Simply start with one of them, for example the *Lying Leopard TTouch* or the *Abalone*, and gradually widen your repertoire. Try to discover which TTouch your cat enjoys most.

Some cats are so fascinated by TTouch that they will sit entranced watching a TTouch video. It seems as though they actually understand what they are seeing.

The Golden Rule for Cats

Cats enrich our lives by giving us their total love and companionship in so very many ways. You can return the gift by observing "The Golden Rule for Cats," and treating your cat just as you would like to be treated yourself. This includes offering healthy, preservative-free food; fresh, clear water; a cozy bed (which can also be your own); and an annual visit to the vet for a check-up. While there, it's also a good idea to ask for a blood test to check on the status of your cat's immune system.

Case History
A Cat that Enjoys Videos

A brief report: my cat loves to lie sprawled out on her back and

watch the video, *Tellington Training for Dogs* video. The video fascinates her. *Axel*

Cats as Companions

Many people who live alone, both young and old, are delighted to have the affectionate company of an animal friend—and a cat is an ideal pet, particularly for people who live in the city. Nevertheless, many cats don't like sitting on a lap or being stroked for longer than a minute. This can be frustrating for some cat owners, who wind up asking themselves whether there is something

wrong with the way they are dealing with their capricious pet.

With TTouch, cats become gentle and affectionate companions who take pleasure in closeness with humans. At the same time, owners who use TTouch to give warmth and affection to their cats are actually contributing to their own health and contentment. Scientific studies have shown that people in close relationships with animal companions have lower blood pressure, a more stable immune system, and are less stressed and generally healthier than those who do not.

Thus, the caring time spent "TTouching" one's cat becomes a special "wellness experience"

Total relaxation, happy purring, excellent balance—you can achieve all this for your cat with the TTouches.

TTouchTip *T*

- ▸ **Chimp** TTouch p. 72
- ▸ **Combination** TTouch p. 83
- ▸ **Ear** TTouch p. 94
- ▸ **Mouth** TTouch p. 98
- ▸ **Tail** TTouch p. 109

with positive effects that are felt by both human and purring friend.

TTouch for the Whole Family

Is there a cat in your family? If so, it is definitely worthwhile for you to familiarize yourself and your loved ones with the TTouch. Not only does learning the TTouch create joy, it also establishes a basis for a much closer bond of trust between human and cat: TTouching truly does offer more than stroking!

Discover the well-being that can radiate from your own hands. Get to know your cat better and help him to enjoy a healthier, happier and longer life. For centuries, people have intuitively known that loving caregiving strengthens the immune system and quickens the life force, and today this knowledge has become scientific fact. TTouch provides

You'll be surprised at the miracles your hands can perform. The TTouch introduces a completely new way to handle your animal companion.

many of the above positive effects, and enriches the life of every responsible cat owner.

Once you have become familiar with TTouch, you can then show your family members how to pamper your feline friend and be rewarded with loud and appreciative purring. Through TTouch, anyone can develop a close and special relationship with a cat.

Actually, it's preferable to try the TTouches out on each other first, so that you can develop a sense of the various levels of pressure, and experience for yourself the feelings of comfort the method brings. Remember that cats need and enjoy a much lighter TTouch than humans. The lightest pressure on the TTouch scale is Number One—this corresponds to the softest possible contact on the eyelid. The Number Three pressure is twice as strong as Number One.

Cats and Children

Taking the time to teach children TTouch results in many benefits for both children and cats. Through TTouch, a child has a way of developing a special and intense relationship with an animal.

We know many children who have learned how to do the TTouch very quickly and also know intuitively how to make the correct movements. Too, children are often more sensitive and more spontaneous than adults, which works in their favor. When shy children establish a strong relationship with an animal, they often become more self-confident. Learning the TTouch frequently calms and relaxes overactive children, since its positive effects also include the "Toucher." The circling movement of the hand has an unusually positive effect on brain waves. Another plus, it takes only a few minutes a day of TTouch to develop a deeper relationship with an animal.

By connecting with a different kind of playmate than they are accustomed to, children learn to be respectful and attentive. Usually, cats like being with

TTouchTip **T**

▸ **Raccoon TTouch p. 74**
▸ **Abalone TTouch p. 62**

children and enjoy their company. If, however, your cat is afraid of children, TTouch can help him become more tolerant of the rough handling kids sometimes innocently inflict. When children are too young to respect a cat's needs, they should be kept away at a safe distance.

Building Self-Confidence Through TTouch

Rolf still vividly remembers the time when he thought he was going to have to part with his cat, Max. When his sister, Sonja, was born, Max's personality underwent a complete change. He could be seen only at mealtimes, when after frantically devouring his food, he would slink off. Once in a while, he would actually allow himself to take a nap in the cat basket, but at the sound of Sonja's voice, he would start up nervously and take immediate, panicky flight. The prospect of ever bringing Sonja and Max together seemed hopeless.

Rolf and his mother went to the vet for advice, telling him about the intolerable situation and his fear that the only way out would be to give up his cat. The vet, however, had a different solution:

he recommended TTouch work for Max. This cat clearly lacked self-confidence, and TTouch work would be a marvelous way to help him regain it.

Taking this advice to heart, Rolf began by working on Max with *Ear* and *Lying Leopard TTouches*. At first, the cat reacted to the contact by backing away, so Rolf switched to using the back of his hand to make the circles we call the *Llama TTouch*, which Max was better able to accept. After a time, Rolf was able to do TTouches over Max's entire body, and was delighted to see his cat stretch out and visibly relax.

From then on, Rolf worked with his cat in daily sessions of five to ten minutes of TTouch circles, activating Max's body's cells to release deep-seated fear. Max increasingly gained self-confidence, and soon, Rolf reported, he once more took time to eat his food, and even remained in the living room when Sonja was playing in her playpen.

The TTouches helped to restore the cat's self-image and overcome his fears. Today, Max lies on the living room couch purring, and even allows Sonja to scratch his back. It's hard to believe that only

T *TTouchTip*

▸ Ear
   TTouch p. 94
▸ Lying Leopard
   TTouch p. 64
▸ Llama TTouch
   p. 70
▸ Hair Slides p. 90

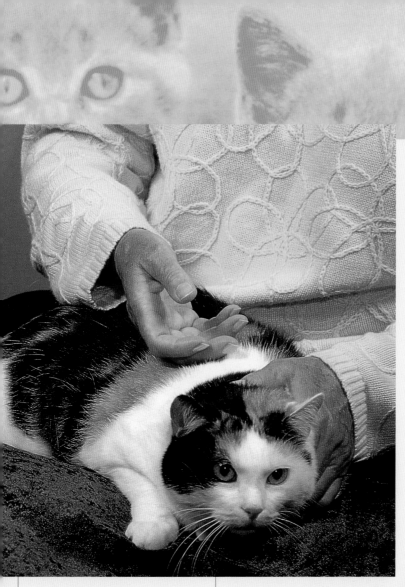

Sometimes, particularly sensitive cats are more comfortable if you use the back of your hand during their first encounter with TTouch.

TTouchTip (T)

▸ **Combination TTouch p. 83**
▸ **Raccoon TTouch p. 74**
▸ **Tarantula TTouch p. 87**

a few months earlier their relationship was marked by insecurity and distrust. When Sonja is somewhat older, she too will learn to spoil her four-legged friend with TTouches.

A Kitten Moves In

The big day has arrived. At last, you are bringing your new kitten home! However, although you rejoice on the occasion, it can sometimes mean distress and separation anxiety for the little cat. From one moment to the next, he is suddenly separated from his mother and siblings. His first human contact and caregiver is now gone and his familiar environment is suddenly replaced by the inside of a car. Such a shock can be hard for a kitten to digest. With the help of TTouch, your new companion will be able to master this first major crisis of his life more easily.

Stress-Free Travel

Cats are often frightened when they go for their first car trip, whether it is to the vet, to a cat show, or just for a journey. Some meow the entire time, their paws sweating with fear. Others jump into the car and enjoy the trip from the outset. In any case, arranging a safe journey for your cat is important. Even if your cat is safely stowed in a carrier, you should have a second person with you to do the driving, so that you are able to spend some time TTouching your cat. When you first get into the car, remain parked for five to ten minutes while you do *Ear Strokes* and other TTouches. If, when underway, your cat is restless,

make a few stops and give him reassuring TTouches.

If you are planning a longer journey and your cat is a nervous traveler, prepare him by taking a few short, introductory trips with stops for TTouch to help avoid motion sickness. The *Ear TTouch* works very well in preventing the nausea that comes with car-sickness.

Even if you think that you don't need to contain your cat in a carrier because he is calm and quiet when traveling, please learn from the following experience of a friend of mine. Her cat dearly loved to travel and my friend always allowed her the freedom of the car. One day, the cat slipped under the brake pedal just as my friend was approaching a stop sign. To avoid hurting her cat, she didn't brake and wound up colliding with an oncoming vehicle. So, please be careful, and invest in a carrier. You should get one with a window so that your cat can look out and around, and also see you when you talk to him. If you're patient and practice the TTouches when traveling by car, it's more than likely that you'll overcome his fears.

T *TTouchTip*

▸ Ear TTouch
   p. 94
▸ Combination
   TTouch p. 83
▸ Tarantula
   TTouch p. 87

The First Hours in a New Home

A cat that has just arrived in a new home needs time and peace to inspect his new living quarters. Therefore, on the first day, it's advisable not to let friends and relatives make a huge fuss over this adorable creature that has entered your life. Your new pet must first orient himself and become acquainted with his environment. Here too, TTouches can be of help.

Whether the adventurous newcomer immediately begins to explore his surroundings, or whether he prefers a little nap first depends entirely on his temperament and condition. If the kitty is stressed, do a short treatment with light TTouches.

If you have brought home a young cat that is depressed by the loss of his mother, siblings, and former home, this is the ideal moment to gain his trust with TTouch. Often, this will help a kitten to calm down, feel welcome and by the next day even demand further TTouches from his new family.

TTouchTip T

- ▸ **Combination TTouch p. 83**
- ▸ **Ear TTouch p. 94**
- ▸ **Hair Slides p. 90**
- ▸ **Slow, Lying Leopard TTouches p. 64**
- ▸ **Python TTouch p. 82**

With the help of TTouch, your little kitten will quickly feel happy in his new home, and will gladly give you his whole heart.

For the next fifteen to twenty years, you will be taking complete responsibility for your cat. The TTouch can help to enhance the beauty and intimacy of these years.

Health and Well-Being

Silky, shining fur, radiant clear eyes, firm claws, healthy white teeth, and a temperament overflowing with joy are sure signs of a cat in blooming good health. Cats show us exactly how they feel, whether they are in overall good condition or whether something is oppressing their sensitive souls. Signs of health problems: your cat may eat less; sleep more; become less active; or lose his usual zest for living. Loving your "little domesticated tiger" also means that you gladly take on the responsibility of

keeping him healthy and happy for the next fifteen, or even twenty, years. The TTouch is there to help you contribute to a healthier, stronger, and longer life.

Once you've experienced the sight of your cat all stretched out, totally relaxed, and purring loudly while you pamper him with *Lying Leopard TTouches*, and once you've felt his small head press against your hand to encourage you to move on to the *Ear TTouch*, it will be completely clear to you that for kitty, TTouches are akin to bliss.

TTouch increases general well-being while at the same time strengthening the bond of trust between human and animal. Its health benefits are also obvious: when one is really healthy, the body's defense system is automatically strengthened and many potential illnesses are, so to speak, stopped cold before they start. So, if you TTouch your cat regularly, you are not only actively supporting his health, you are also effectively helping to prevent acute and chronic illnesses and increase your cat's life expectancy. It's a known fact that when all beings are deeply loved, cared for, and spoiled with physical as well as mental

stroking, they live longer and remain healthier.

Unaltered Male Cats

The neutering of male cats is a much discussed topic, and one that has prompted many an experienced owner to ask themselves if it is fair or kind to try to integrate an unaltered male into normal family life. Though most experienced breeders would find it difficult to answer this question with an unequivocal yes, TTouch can provide new ways to bring temporary relief to the unfortunate male feline in his difficult situation.

An unaltered male displays many undesirable behavior patterns: Spraying causes a very unpleasant odor; there is always the risk that he will father unwanted kittens; and he is harder to handle than his neutered counterpart—the appeal of the opposite sex is almost always more interesting to him than the two-legged friend attempting to win the honor of his attention with all sorts of goodies.

*Do the TTouch on your "stud" cat with
the help of a soft sheepskin cloth.*

A young male in particular, is driven by high hormonal energy, causing him to spray often and to need a relatively large amount of sexual activity in order to maintain a cheerful frame of mind. Interestingly enough, TTouch can positively influence this hormonal roller coaster and lift the cat's depressed spirits. TTouches also give him greater emotional and physical equilibrium and allow him to be more affectionate with humans.

It's definitely better to keep an unaltered male separate from the rest of the cat population. This can make it difficult to take care of the cat's needs and also your own, because you should set aside at least two to three hours daily to dedicate fully and completely to the cat so that he will not become depressed from his isolated life. If you are at home all day, it's probably not too hard to find a way to schedule a cat TTouch session in between other tasks. But, even if you are short of time, it's important not to deprive your cat of the good effects that TTouches bring.

If you need to separate him from other cats, a good solution is to give him a neutered male for

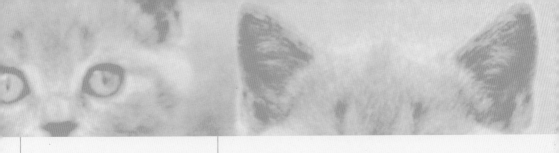

companionship. To avoid jealousy, do TTouch on both cats in each other's presence. If you plan to mate the cat with a female living in the house, temporarily remove the neutered cat to other quarters so that the two males don't become aggressive with each other. After the mating is over, the "male-bonding" should resume without problems. However, if difficulties between them arise, TTouches can be employed to defuse the situation.

▸ **Case History**
Incontinent Behavior
I must report what a terrific success we've had using TTouch: Alan's friend blamed herself because her cat—for no apparent reason—urinated in every conceivable corner of the house. Alan told her about the TTouch and suggested she try it at least once. "It can't do any harm and perhaps it might even help," he told her. When she saw Alan again one week later, she told him she had tried TTouches on the cat, who loved them, and as a result, the cat now followed her around everywhere wanting to be TTouched. Alan asked whether the

cat was still incontinent. The woman said no, and that since she had used the TTouch, the cat no longer urinated anywhere in the house. *Nancy and Alan Smith*

The Breeding Visit

When a female cat, the queen, arrives for a breeding visit, TTouches can help her to feel comfortable more quickly in the unfamiliar surroundings. Breeders often find that planned matings are unsuccessful because the nerves of the couple "involved" are on edge. You can prevent such frustrating experiences by making the cats as comfortable as possible and strengthening their self-assurance with the TTouches you find listed here.

TTouchTip (T)

▸ Ear
  TTouch p. 94
▸ Raccoon
  TTouch on the
  legs and paws
  p. 74
▸ Belly Lift
  p. 101
▸ Abalone TTouch
  over the whole
  body p. 62
▸ Lying Leopard
  TTouches on
  the belly, inside
  and outside the
  legs, and on
  the paws p. 64
▸ Tail
  TTouch p. 109

Mothers and Kittens

Approximately three to four weeks later, you can usually tell whether the cat has conceived. You can see swellings in the abdomen that are actually tiny, maturing kittens. Her nipples gradually turn pink and noticeably stand out from her body. The fur around the nipples slowly recedes, so that later, the hungry kittens will have no problem gaining access to their mother's nurturing milk. Altogether, it takes sixty-three to sixty-five days before the new generation finally sees the light of the world.

Though every pregnancy is different, there are some changes that you can observe in nearly all expectant cats. The mother-to-be will exhibit an increasing attachment to her caregiver and seek out the company of her human companion, asking for extra amounts of stroking and affection. This is an ideal time to use light TTouches on her sides.

Several days before the birth, some cats will exhibit further changes in behavior. Her newly altered hormonal state can stimulate a strong caregiving instinct that often manifests as intense licking of other beings. If no other cats are present in the household, plush toys or even the family dog can become the object of this intense maternal cleaning. If the licking degenerates into a downright cleaning frenzy, you can help her relax by doing *Lying Leopard TTouches*.

Should your cat trust you so much that she chooses to give birth in your presence, you can work on her between contractions with relaxing TTouches. As soon as the contractions begin, support your cat's back with your hand— many cats seem to find this extremely helpful. If the birth is long or difficult, do *Ear TTouches*, slow, *Lying Leopard TTouches*, and *Python TTouches* on the abdominal area.

After the cat and her new litter recover from the strain of birth and have been given some peace with enough time to become acquainted, you'll find many appropriate uses for TTouches. They help to restore strength, reinforce the connection between mother and kittens, and also fortify the bond of trust with humans. It's also a good idea to

T **TTouchTip**

▸ Ear
  TTouch p. 94
▸ Abalone
  TTouch p. 62

introduce the kittens to TTouch—in fact, it's important, because it will help them develop into adult cats that approach humans with trust and friendliness.

Mastitis To be a responsible breeder, you must continue to watch for any problems that can arise. In many cases, should there be complications, you can—in consultation with your vet—be an active participant in the care of your cat and kittens. For instance, you can aid in problems with nursing.

Although things usually proceed normally after birth, sometimes an inflammation of the milk glands, known as mastitis, can suddenly flare up causing the milk to stop flowing freely and to back up internally. The entire suckling area is distinctly more prominent, and feels swollen and hard to the touch. Other typical symptoms of this disease are redness and heat in the area. In the advanced stage, blue-red or black-violet discolorations appear. At worst, there may even be dead tissue, known as necrosis. Obviously, backed-up milk and resulting inflammation are extremely painful so the condition should be treated as quickly as possible. Veterinarians usually prescribe antibiotics and a healing salve. You can also support the healing process: After first consulting with your vet, take a warm, wet

The TTouch is an excellent way to ease a stressed show cat.

T *TTouchTip*

▸ Raccoon
TTouch P. 74

cloth and make tiny, two-second *Raccoon TTouches* (Number One pressure). These measures should enable the stream of milk to once again flow freely.

Stars of the Show — Large and Small

It's seven o'clock in the morning, a cool, refreshing breeze wafts through the streets. People holding cat carriers crowd the narrow entrance of the exhibition hall. From many show booths comes the sound of the meowing and hissing of cats upset by all the commotion. Irma rubs her eyes. This is her first cat show. "It's stressful," she grumbles, but still, she's pleased that over the last few weeks she has taken the time to strengthen the nervous system of her cat, Aline, with the assistance of various TTouches.

The vet arrives and Aline willingly allows her to apply the stethoscope and examine her eyes and ears. This "ingénue" is behaving like a true professional. "Thank goodness we practiced calming the whole body with TTouch," Irma says. Other cats have retreated into their carriers. No, they will not willingly get onto the big examination table! However, the friendly vet is experienced and also familiar with TTouch: she calms the nervous cats down with gentle *Ear TTouches* and they are soon examined.

The exhibition hall continues to buzz with activity. Over three hundred cats must be accommodated. The owners disinfect the cages and decorate them with mats and small curtains. Aline is somewhat nervous. She darts curiously around her cage. New toys—a plush mouse and a rubber ball—hold no interest, however, after the *Ear TTouch*, she calms down and makes herself comfortable despite the hectic atmosphere.

At last, it's Aline's turn. Irma quickly picks up the brush for a final pass at Aline's tail and coat, gives her cat a soothing, last minute *Hair Slide*, and then the decisive moment is at hand. The judge views the young Norwegian cat with a critical eye. Breed, head, ears, tail, quality of fur, and size and color of the eyes are all considered. The judge is satisfied. Aline is nominated as "Best in Show," and a few hours later is "presented" on the large exhibition stage. "If I hadn't used stress-relieving TTouches prior to the show to prepare my cat, I'm sure the presentation would not have gone nearly as well," Irma says.

By six o'clock, humans and animals alike are tired. Cage decorations are swiftly removed, and cats are once again ensconced in carriers. An arduous day is at an end. "Once we're home, I'll take a little more time to do TTouches on Aline." Irma says. "Then the stress of this exciting day will be truly be over." She waves goodbye.

▶ **Case History**
Improving Show-time Performance
Some time ago, I visited the Cat Fanciers' International Cat Show in Hayward, California. I was there to inform as many exhibitors as possible about TTouch and to explain to them that TTouch is a helpful way for them to increase the health and the beauty of their cats. Loudspeakers broadcast an invitation to come and learn the TTouch in a private session, and I spoke with many exhibitors personally. I worked with both short and longhaired cats—predominantly Ragdoll, Abyssinian, Burmese, and Maine Coon breeds.

Most exhibitors had heard of the TTouch, but didn't really have any idea of what the method is all about. In the midst of an exciting and arduous day at the show, they

TTouchTip Ⓣ

▸ **Ear TTouch p. 94**
▸ **Tarantula TTouch p. 87**
▸ **Hair Slides p. 90**

were curious to see whether the TTouch could actually relax their stressed-out cats in only a few minutes.

I showed participants different TTouches: *Noah's March*, the *Ear TTouch*, the *Tail TTouch*, *Belly Lifting*, the *Tarantula TTouch,* and *Hair Slides.* I explained to people that they should pay attention to their animal's reaction to the TTouches: licking; head turning from one side to the other; stretching out forelegs that had been tucked under the body; a content expression in the eye; an erect posture of the body; a tail held high; outstretched hind legs; the body relaxed when lying down; and exposing the belly.

I explained that just two-minute sessions of TTouch daily, beginning with *Ear TTouches*, can improve performance in a show substantially, because among other things, it prepares the cat to be handled by the steward and the judge.

I asked each person to try the TTouch on her cat and personally witness how the expression in the eyes changed completely in spite of the restless atmosphere in the exhibition hall. It was such a pleasure for me to observe these owners concentrating on their breathing, trying to determine which pressures were best, and which TTouches were most appropriate for their cats.

I made it clear to the exhibitors, how important it is at the end to allow the animal an extra two-to-five minute rest period after doing the TTouches. This permits any stress to totally dissipate. The *Ear TTouch* was particularly enthusiastically received because it clearly brought the quickest results. When the exhibition reached its high point in the late afternoon, the performances of the cats that had taken part in the earlier TTouch sessions, were

Prepare your show cat for the judge with TTouches.

ample proof of its effectiveness.

A cat that had objected to being moved from her sleeping mat with loud hissing that morning received a better rating than she ever had in any previous show. It had always been a traumatic experience for her to be placed on the judging table, and usually, the owner had to hold the cat because she would not allow the judge to touch her. This time, however, it was an entirely different story. She permitted the judge to place her into position without hissing, and observed the judge's every movement with calm attention.

To see such progress and to experience how effectively TTouch worked for the show's participants was very rewarding. *Anne Snowball, TTEAM Practitioner*

Adopting Animal-Shelter Cats

TTouch helps animal-shelter cats gain security and self-confidence.

Adopting a cat from an animal shelter is, without doubt, a good thing to do, and often a way to make a feline friend, who, after a few days, can become your pal. Unfortunately, however, there is also a negative side. People who can't resist the pleading eyes of a shelter animal, may find after a few weeks, that they can't deal with their new family member. The sad result is that many adopted cats are abandoned and end up right back in the shelter.

The situation of a cat that has been through such an experience has now gotten worse. Yet again, he has experienced a breach of trust: the loss of a caregiver, another change of environment, disorientation. The effect of his original trauma is magnified by every new occurrence of this sort. Many cats react with behavior problems such as fear, aggression, incontinence, and a deep-seated distrust of humans.

If you have adopted such a cat or are toying with the idea of doing so, the TTouch can help to overcome initial difficulties. Play some calm music to create a relaxed atmosphere, sit on your sofa or a comfortable chair, and with the cat held securely but without constraint between your legs, work on him with TTouch. Such calm togetherness can dissolve the cat's fear at the same time as it weaves the first strand in a bond between you and this frightened soul. If your cat cannot bear being close to humans, it is often helpful to wrap a towel around his chest that you can hold closed at the back of his neck while you do TTouches through the towel. To give the cat a feeling of security, make sure that all four feet remain grounded. Work on him for several sessions, but only for a few minutes each time, using the *Clouded Leopard TTouch* with a Number One pressure on both

sides of the back, and the *Abalone TTouch* along the flanks. Do *Raccoon TTouches* down the legs to the paw pads to reduce fear and to encourage the cat to allow body contact. If your cat is very frightened, be careful to wrap him in the towel in such a way so that you cannot be bitten. Read more about this topic on page 37.

TTouch in the Animal Shelter

Many people who work in animal shelters around the world have reported to us how valuable TTouch is to them in their work. They describe how heartening it is for both humans and animals, especially when the caregivers find themselves working under high pressure with little time to spare for any one animal. Just two or three minutes of purposeful and concentrated TTouch can make an enormous difference to an animal. If, through TTouch, you can help cats to regain self-confidence and to reduce their fear and aggression step by step, you'll be aiding them to become more adoptable, thus assuring

T *TTouchTip*

- Clouded Leopard TTouch p. 67
- Abalone TTouch p. 62
- Raccoon TTouch p. 74
- Chimp TTouch p. 72

some of the cats home temporarily. After I learned about the TTouch, I wanted to try it out on our "foster-cat children." The way their difficult behavior changed was hard to believe. In all the years since we first started taking in cats, I have never seen anything like it. It's amazing to see how TTouch can improve, and even solve, problems of body and spirit. *Karen Stoklosa, DVM*

Anxious cats will often become more trusting if you wrap them in a soft towel.

one more cat a new and happy family life.

Case History
Foster Cats

I work for an organization that is responsible for catching stray cats and sheltering them. Over the past eight years, over eight hundred cats have been picked up. Some of them are not adoptable, because they are feral or shy, and will not allow anyone to touch them. At this time, there are seventy-six cats living in the shelter, including kittens that are the least adoptable, having learned from their mothers to mistrust humans.

My family and I help out the shelter by occasionally taking

TTouch in Veterinary Practice

Interview with
Oliver C. Schmid, DVM

Have you been practicing veterinary medicine for a long time?

Since 1990. The first three years I worked in an animal hospital, then I went into independent practice.

Which animals come to your practice most frequently?

Cats and dogs, of course, and different popular domestic animals such as rabbits and guinea pigs.

What are the most typical difficulties for cats when visiting the vet?

TTouchTip (T)

- **Any TTouch that the cat finds enjoyable**
- **Chimp TTouch p. 72**
- **Noah's March p. 80**
- **Circles with the point of a "wand" in front of the cat (see p. 48)**

More and more vets use TTouch in their practices to calm their four-legged patients.

Many cats react very well to the Ear TTouch, which is a useful aid when traveling or waiting for the vet.

Many cats are very fearful, while others react downright aggressively. I am also frequently presented with animals that become withdrawn and shy, attempt to escape, tremble all over, or strike at me with a paw. I often see many owners who have no influence over their cats and are extremely anxious themselves. Many cats even begin to suffer strain and fear in the waiting room.

For what kind of cases have you successfully used TTouches?

I've had excellent results using *Ear TTouch* for anxious cats. Especially sensitive animals react

well to the *Abalone TTouch*, or can be reassured by the *Llama TTouch* that nothing threatening is about to happen. As soon as my patients are somewhat calmer, I try to win their confidence with gentle *Clouded Leopard TTouches*.

How did you discover and learn TTouch?

I first saw Linda Tellington-Jones demonstrate her method in the mid 1970's at "Equitana," the big horse exhibition in Essen, Germany. I tried TTouch and had great success using the technique with horses. The equine world had been employing TTouch for many years, and so as a veterinarian, it made sense to me to try it on other animals. After the outstanding response of my own dogs, I began using TTouch with

the cats that were brought to my practice—sometimes with amazing success.

On what do you base your belief in the positive effects of TTouch?

TTouch promotes contact between humans and animals, which in turn strengthens trust. The method creates well-being by uniting closeness with useful training methods. The cat learns to entrust himself to human hands, and in time, comes to accept situations like a visit to the vet with a great deal more ease. The cat owner pays more attention to his animal and learns how to handle him in a stress-free way. I also consider it quite possible that TTouch has therapeutic effects—TTouch can't do any harm, and it may actually help.

What other animals do you do the TTouches on?

Dogs and horses. Many dogs react extremely positively to *Lying Leopard TTouches*, and gladly allow *Raccoon TTouches* on sensitive areas of the body. I've found that the *Python TTouch* works very successfully on horses that don't like contact with their legs. I like using the *Tarantula TTouch* to stimulate circulation.

Which TTouches do you particularly recommend to cat owners?

I heartily recommend the *Ear TTouch* because most cats take great pleasure in it, and it's also a good starting point from which to introduce other TTouches. I always advise *Lying Leopard TTouches* on the back and belly area, but TTouches on the tail and paws require great care because many cats simply will not tolerate them.

What are the limits for the TTouch?

In veterinary practice, there's usually no opportunity to apply TTouch to hyper-aggressive or extremely panicked cats. And as far as therapeutic success is

Profile:
Name: Oliver C. Schmid, DVM
Born: April 21, 1961 in Bonn, Germany
Training: 1985–1990: student of veterinary medicine at the Veterinary University, Hannover, Germany
Doctoral Thesis: The Therapeutic Use of Healing Plants in Veterinary Practice, 1994
Professional Practice 1990–1994: assistant physician in an animal hospital. 1994 to the present: own practice in Ratingen-Lintorf, Germany

concerned, I definitely see limits to its use for degenerative and internal problems. However, in the orthopedic field, TTouches can offer effective support.

Case History
A Veterinarian Recommends TTouch

I recommend the use of TTouch to nearly all cat owners. If you have a kitten or a puppy, the method teaches you the best way to touch them. It can also help with behavioral problems, with the added plus that the animal is relieved from stress. Full-grown animals can also benefit. They simply feel healthier, and the owner becomes aware of painful conditions before problems become chronic.

Older cats—in particular animals with arthritic symptoms, hip dysplasia, disc problems or spondylitis—react extremely well. It helps to ease muscles around the painful areas, which in turn leads to greater mobility. I am convinced that animals remain healthy longer and need fewer visits to the vet when their owners give them regular TTouch sessions. *Stan Goldfarb, DVM*

Case History
Missy Meow—
A Badly Injured Cat

Susanne first brought Missy Meow to the vet with a gaping wound in her foreleg. The entire leg was also rotated with the paw pads facing upward. The cat's body was totally covered with small cuts and other injuries, particularly on her face. X rays showed no fractures so the vet prescribed rest and physio-therapy. But, when the leg showed no improvement, the doctor began to consider amputation.

After four days in Susanne's care, Missy Meow's condition still had not improved. Susanne decided to learn TTouch and almost immediately gave the cat her first TTouch session. The next morning, though Missy's leg was still stiff, its position was a bit better. Susanne continued with *Lying Leopard* and *Raccoon TTouches* and was rewarded with astonishing success, which she joyously reported to us: "After one week of TTouch work and physiotherapy, Missy's leg returned to its original position. Progress continued in the following weeks until, at last,

Health Care for Cats

Inoculations
Shows and journeys: mandatory and suggested inoculations
Preparatory TTouches: Ear TTouch, Chimp TTouch

Claw Trimming
Usually unnecessary for young, active cats. Needed for older and ill cats that no longer wear down their claws.
Preparatory TTouches: Raccoon TTouch and Paw TTouch

Ear Care
Occasional cleaning of the outside ear flap. For this, use either a special ear cleaner or a damp cloth; do not clean down inside the ear as this may cause injury.
Preparatory TTouch: Ear TTouch

Dental Care
Regular tartar control by the vet, healthy nutrition
Preparatory TTouches: Mouth TTouch and Gum TTouch

Intimate Care After Self-Soiling
For extreme cases: use a damp cloth, wash with mild shampoo, baby powder to dry the area
Preparatory TTouches: Tail TTouch, Raccoon TTouch, Lying Leopard TTouch on the hind legs.

Parasites
For outdoor cats: fleas, ticks, mites, worms. Solutions: On-the-spot removal, flea collar and other anti-flea preparations
Preparatory TTouch: Hair Slides

Worm Cures
For outdoor cats: four times per year. For indoor cats: no more than twice a year.
Preparatory TTouches: Mouth TTouch and Gum TTouch

Preparation for a Visit to the Vet: all stress-reducing TTouches

Missy could once more move her leg and paw. Though she still sometimes limps, she can now run up and down the stairs with no problem, use the cat box, and even jump onto the window sill to look out at the world." *Vera*

When a Cat Reaches the Senior Years

In growing old, we humans are not the only ones to often encounter mounting health problems: cats that have passed the zenith of their lives can also suffer increasingly from certain debilitating illnesses.

On the average, older cats get sick more frequently than the young, but not as often as old dogs, by far. Even twenty-year-old cats frequently do not become senile, and usually remain relatively active.

Nevertheless, certain changes cannot be denied: cats lose body mass, while fatty tissue tends to increase. Connective tissue, and nerve and muscle cells are in decline. Further consequences of the natural aging process are: a slowed metabolism; diminished circulation and digestion; tooth problems; and a lessened ability to heal. This is exactly the time for you to support and activate your cat's vitality with TTouch sessions—even if only for five minutes.

Aging is not a disease in and of itself, but a physiological development. The body is simply no longer able to assimilate the interior and exterior onslaughts of daily life. With the help of TTouch, you can strengthen your cat's immune system. Unfortunately, chronic diseases can pile up in older cats, creating a fertile ground for further illness. If you TTouch your four-legged friend daily, you can lessen the chances of him contracting chronic illnesses.

The aging process cannot be stopped. However, you can do a lot to create as pleasant an environment as possible. Besides TTouch, it's important that your cat receives the kind of nutrition that meets his individual needs and also that he has ample opportunity for active movement. *Ear TTouches* and *Belly Lifts* can prevent or sooth digestive difficulties. It's important too, to take your "senior" cat to the vet for regular check-ups.

T TTouchTip

▸ TTouches your cat enjoys performed lightly and slowly.
▸ Ear TTouch to strengthen the immune system. p. 94

TTouches can help your senior cat stay healthy and happy, and live a longer life.

The Last Good-bye

Unfortunately, not even the most loving care can change the fact that one day the time will finally arrive when cat and owner must look into each other's eyes for the last time. Acute and chronic illnesses, severe injuries or accidents as well as other unforeseeable internal and external events can shorten the precious lifespan of most cats. Thus, overweight cats and outdoor cats that dart across heavily trafficked roads, will clearly have a shorter life span than cats of normal weight who live a protected life inside the home.

When the moment of final parting arrives, many cat owners feel deeply despondent and helpless. They burst into a flood of tears at the vet clinic or stand, overcome, beside their beloved cat's bed, not knowing how to cope with the situation.

The TTouch offers you something you can do in this most difficult moment. Doing slow (three-second) *Abalone TTouches* with long pauses, supports your animal's soul as it takes leave of the body. Don't make fast, heavy, or small circles because they may disturb or interrupt this phase. When you say this last goodbye, it's perfectly all right to cry. Let

your cat know how much you love and will miss him, but also tell him that you understand that it's his time to go. Say to him that he will have your love forever. This is the time to release your cat to begin his journey to the other side.

Letting go can be very difficult. Many years ago, I was asked to do TTouch on a fifteen-year-old cat with laryngeal cancer that could hardly breathe anymore. I felt that this animal was only alive because his owner could not release him and didn't want to think about life without his cat.

Guilt feelings can also make it hard to let go. I think it's important to be grateful to your cat, and put any guilt feelings aside, because he will forgive you, regardless of what might have happened. If you are able to sit beside your cat at home, supporting him in his last hours, make it a calm time to be together alone. Imagine that the soul of your cat is present close beside you. Use this chance to speak to your cat and thank him for all that he gave to you and to your life.

If your cat must be put to sleep, ask the vet to do so at your home.

Before he comes, plan a ceremony. Light candles and play quiet, serene music. Express all your love to your cat with light, gentle TTouches. Tell him what is going to happen and how very much you will miss him. Grieve for him in the way that is best for him. Imagine your cat crossing a rainbow on the way to heaven, where he will wait for you, well and happy again.

TTouchTip T

▶ **Slow, light Abalone TTouches with long pauses p. 62**

with *TTouch*

Your cat likes to be petted, but only when he feels like it—does this sound familiar? TTouch makes it possible for you to be on closer terms with your cat in a new and gentle way. You'll discover that your feline companion will enjoy relaxing with you almost any time, and that TTouch is as beneficial for you as it is for your cat.

First Contact

When you TTouch your four-legged roommate for the first time, it will probably be easy because you and your cat already know each other well. However, if you are working with a cat that is new, you need to be able to interpret body language. Observe the animal and try to see whether his behavior is open and friendly or inclined toward mistrusting. The cat's body signals will provide the clues.

This shorthaired, domestic cat, Krummel, finds TTouching with the back of the fingers less threatening.

When working with an aggressive cat for the first time, it's best to wrap him in a towel.

Gentle Ear TTouches calm a particularly nervous cat and also create a good basis for trust.

Typical Cat Language

A friendly gaze, ears pointing forward and an upright tail denote a pleasant mood. A twitching tail, striking out, dilated pupils and staring eyes, raised fur along the ridge of the spine, angled or flattened ears, hissing or growling are all warnings that trouble is on the way.

I've been amazed to find, in countless TTouch sessions, that when a cat changes his body signals, his behavior changes as well. If a cat is fearful or aggressive, proceed carefully and don't court danger by trying to hold him. Being heroic helps neither you nor the cat. Instead, see which approach is most easily accepted. Some cats react well to reassuring coaxing, others feel safer snuggled under a soft towel. Sometimes, you can calm an anxious cat by the way you hold your own body and by your gestures. When you lower your eyes, turn your face sideways, lick your lips, and blink, you are sending reassuring signals. Breathe quietly and softly and whisper simple, soothing words. This nonverbal language helps the cat begin to feel comfortably safe again.

Stay Right Here!

If it's your first time working with a cat that has never experienced TTouch and doesn't know how good it feels, you may have to keep him from running away. Apply the same basic rule you do on first meeting a cat you don't know. Be on the safe side—any

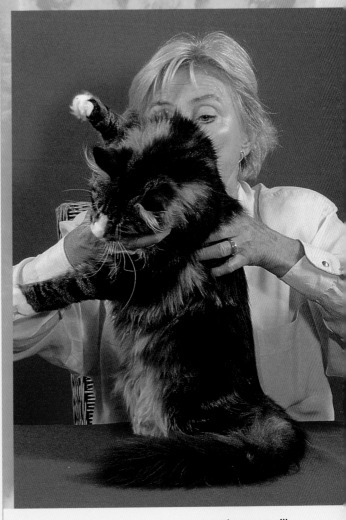

Sometimes, a cat will react defensively at the first touch. Don't let this put you off.

scratch is one scratch too many—not to mention a painful bite.

There are different ways of preventing a cat from running away without resorting to force. Don't try to hold him by hanging on for dear life, but rather see if you can create a situation in which he feels safe and secure and no longer wishes to run away. Experiment to find out which method works best. Keep a sharp eye on your cat so that you can recognize unwelcome reactions before they become problematic. Be gentle but persistent.

Various Holding Methods

Lift your cat onto a table and position him so that he is standing sideways to you. Hold him supportively with one hand under the chest. The index finger of your holding hand rests between his forelegs, while your thumb lies parallel to the shoulder joint. Your cat's hindquarters are tucked between the crook of your elbow and your body, allowing him to lean into you and giving him a sense of safety and security. Should your cat find the contact pleasurable, lean into him lightly with your upper body—this provides an even

LEFT: *I am trying the towel to give this extremely anxious cat a sense of security.*
RIGHT: *But, if the towel threatens the cat, it's better to use your hands.*

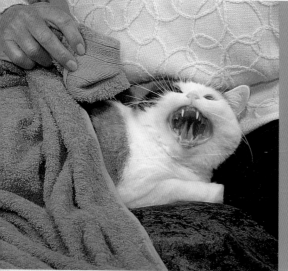
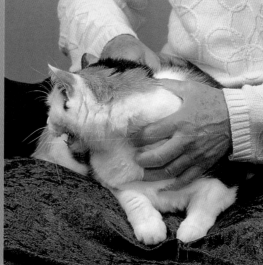

If a cat so completely mistrusts humans that he becomes defensive to the point of extreme aggression, try working on him with the help of a towel. Place the towel gently over his body. Then, carefully wrap him in it so that you are no longer in danger from his teeth and claws. One hand then grasps the towel at the back of the animal's neck, while the other, placed supportively on his side, gradually executes light TTouches through the towel. Make sure that all four of the cat's feet are grounded, otherwise he may be frightened. Sit down on the sofa or on the floor, and hold the

Here, I am placing my hand supportively under Krummel's chest to give him a greater sense of security.

This cat is gaining a feeling of security by leaning against my body as I steady her with one hand on her chest.

greater sense of warmth and security. Then, make light TTouch circles with your other hand to convince him that you are actually doing something nice for him.

Some cats will not tolerate a hand placed under their chests and react to an index finger placed between their forelegs by making vigorous attempts to scratch you. With such animals, position one hand on the cat's chest, and with your other hand placed sideways on his hindquarters, gradually begin making very light, gentle TTouches.

making gentle TTouches on his body. Most insecure cats respond very well to this method.

However, should your cat prove to be a hard case, you can always fall back on the towel-wrap method to convince him that the TTouch of your hands is something to enjoy.

Occasionally practicing this method of holding your cat is a good way to prepare for cat shows. Here, the Siberian kitten, Newskaja Snowidnie's Elliot, shows how well she can already perform.

cat lightly enclosed in your legs. Have him face forward, so that he can't back out of the towel. This method is also successful with anxious as well as aggressive cats. The towel wrapping gives them a sense of safety and security and helps them to quickly accept the TTouch as something pleasurable.

Another way to use this method is with cats that are by nature calm, but initially don't like the TTouch. Place your cat in the bottom half of his carrier or in a low-sided cardboard box and cover him with a towel, leaving his head peeping out. As soon as the cat feels comfortable under the warmth of the towel, begin

This variation of a hold may look unusual, however, it helps anxious kittens feel safe and secure.

TTouches with Sheepskin

Extremely sensitive and touch-intolerant cats may react with uncertainty the first time they are TTouched. When cats have experienced several owner changes, spent lengthy periods in animal shelters, or have been abused by previous owners, they will frequently react with fear and defensiveness. TTouch can be

This is the Abalone TTouch being applied through a towel. It prepares a cat for contact on the sensitive area of the back, and for the Tail TTouch.

helpful—especially helpful, in fact—in such pitiful cases by renewing trust in humans and aiding in establishing lasting, positive relationships with caregivers.

Of course, backsliding and a resurfacing of mistrust sometimes do occur in cases like this. Nevertheless, continue to have patience and make time to work with your insecure animal. A piece of fleecy sheepskin or the like, can be very helpful in this learning process. Make gentle TTouches using the soft sheepskin. Many cats feel this to be less threatening than the human hand, which they may

This method of holding the cat prevents biting and uncontrolled movements of the head.

ABOVE: *This male cat is finding the first TTouches with the sheepskin a bit unsettling ...*
BELOW : *... but winds up enjoying it to the fullest.*

connect with bad memories. Using a sheepskin for TTouch is a good way to give a cat confidence in the work you are doing with him.

Grooming Your Cat's Fur

Not many cat lovers brush their pets, except those who own longhaired or show cats. Actually, there are benefits for both you and your cat if he learns to enjoy brushing: it will bring you joy and relaxation while promoting the good health of your cat. Brushing also serves as a nice complement to TTouch work.

You'll find there are an unbelievably confusing number of tools for cat care, all with their special uses. It's best to brush longhaired, or somewhat longhaired, cats with a brush that has curved metal bristles; afterward, you can use various combs for the fine work. Persians are among the most care intensive breeds and need daily brushing, while one thorough brushing per week is sufficient for Norwegian Forest cats. Try a natural bristle brush to bring a wonderful gloss to the fur.

Shorthaired breeds with silky coats usually enjoy being groomed with a rubber brush. If a cat has a luxurious undercoat, use a metal brush with bent tines and a blunt-toothed comb, and make

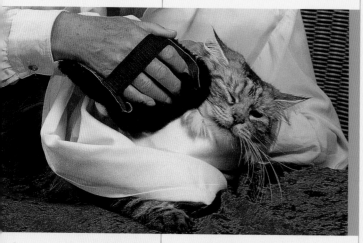

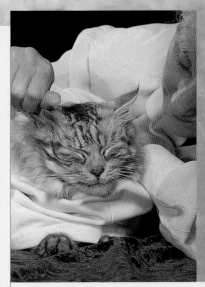

sure not to damage or tear the skin. For breeds without an undercoat, a fine-toothed comb is appropriate.

If you own a Rex cat or similar rare breed, keep in mind that such unusual creatures have extremely sensitive skin. For regular care, use a soft brush or a special rubber pad to avoid injuring or tearing the skin.

So far so good. But what if the cat is not only unimpressed by these wonderful tools, but actually flees at the sight of a brush or comb, or resorts to scratching and biting to send you the clear message that fur care is best left to cats? This unpleasant situation is not exactly a rare occurrence. However, here too, TTouch can be helpful. Accustom your feline to gentle TTouches, for example, *Hair Slides*, and after a time, intersperse the TTouches with the light stroke of a soft brush. After a while, your cat will learn to accept combs and metal brushes—presuming you are sensitive and careful with your grooming technique. Brush slowly and mindfully so that your cat enjoys every stroke. If you keep the sessions short, your cat's resistance to brushing will lessen.

If you neglect the care of your cat's fur, it can become knotted and nappy, creating a perfect habitat for parasites. In addition, unkempt cats are susceptible to skin diseases like psoriasis.

Gloves

Gloves may seem like an odd item to associate with cats. Indeed, I use such aids only rarely, and some people feel, not entirely without justification, that contact with gloves can make a sensitive cat unnecessarily nervous. They certainly have a point if gloves are used thoughtlessly without preparing the cat first, and for the purpose of restraining him. Of course, a cat will be frightened if he is forcibly held down on a treatment table by a pair of huge

gloves and then rewarded with a painful injection.

This scenario is definitely not what I have in mind. I've already stressed that your own safety should always be your first consideration when working with animals. Therefore, when you work with an aggressive cat who is trying to scratch or bite, be sure to take precautionary measures to protect your hands, and if possible, your arms. If you intend to work with a dangerous cat, you should wear gloves while performing TTouches. Soft but thick deerskin gloves are perfectly suited to this purpose because they are supple enough to permit delicate movements, yet thick enough to offer protection from sharp claws and teeth. Take care not to allow an aggressive cat to injure the sensitive area of your wrist.

If there is a chance that you might be bitten or scratched, a good way to protect yourself while accustoming the cat to TTouches is to wear a pair of soft leather gloves. The Exotic Shorthair male "Santa Fe Jewel," reacted with irritation to my using gloves. I proceed particularly carefully with him.

Place one hand on your cat to offer him a sense of stability and security, and use the other to work on him with a mindful TTouch. In your first sessions, proceed very carefully and give your cat the opportunity to get used to the TTouches. At first, he may resist with all his might, however, it won't be long before he gives up his defensive attitude and arrives at a new feeling of well-being and confidence.

As soon as the cat accepts your gloved TTouches without defensive aggression and even begins to enjoy the contact, you can gradually introduce working on him with bare hands.

Now, Jewel is no longer finding the gloves unpleasant.

Strong Cats

1. The cream-colored Burmese, Felix, is not yet convinced that TTouch is a pleasant experience. He hisses in protest and clings to the tablecloth with all four paws.

2. I succeed in convincing Felix that I'm about to do something nice to him. To overcome his defensive reactions, I am steadying him with one hand at his chest, and using the other to do Belly Lifts.

3. Felix does not like surprises. He claws at the sheepskin massage brush and signals with his entire body, "I will not relax, and I don't care one bit about the wonderful things you've planned for me." Felix is mistaken.

4. Loud hissing is Felix's reaction to having his head massaged with the sheepskin brush. Although his behavior still signals a defensive attitude, he has not once attempted to attack me.

5. There now, that wasn't so bad after all! At this point, Felix presses his head against the sheepskin and permits gentle TTouches without a single hiss. His eyes still express supreme self-confidence—a trait that's natural for strong cats like Felix.

6. After a break, I come to say good-bye. He emerges on his own from his carrier, and invites me to play. Felix puts his head in my hand, purring happily. Patience and persistence win out!

TTouches with a Feather

A stiff feather can work true miracles with an anxious or distrustful cat that won't allow TTouch. A turkey or goose feather is good to use, or any other appropriate feather: you can probably find a brightly-colored one in a fashion notions or novelty shop. First, give your cat plenty of time to sniff the feather. Then, test areas of your cat's body to see where he likes being touched with the feather, and gently stroke these areas. If the cat acts annoyed, change your position or the pressure you are using. Some cats enjoy being stroked softly on the head, but be careful not to stroke inside the ear as this can tickle.

You can also use the feather to work on problematic body zones. Many cats don't like to be stroked around the base of the tail or on the hindquarters. Take the feather, stroke lightly a few times over the sensitive area, then make very delicate circles with the feather on the surface of the fur to alleviate the sensitivity. Simultaneously, reassure your cat by talking quietly to him and

Before you begin stroking your cat with a feather, let him sniff it.

LEFT: *At first this Norwegian Forest cat is somewhat irritated...*
RIGHT: *...but she is soon delighted with the sensation of the feather stroking her.*

ABOVE: *Sensitive cats often find strokes with a feather pleasant.*
BELOW: *Even particularly sensitive areas can be touched with a feather, usually without a problem.*

placing your other hand supportively on his chest. If you repeat the gentle, feather TTouches regularly, your cat will gain confidence, and one day will allow you to TTouch him with your bare hands.

Case History
TTouching with a Feather
My two-year-old cat flatly refused to be touched, so I began to use tiny TTouches with a feather on her. Surprisingly, after the first session, she wholeheartedly accepted being softly stroked over her entire body. I repeated the feather TTouch sessions several times to familiarize her with the sensation. She now loves to be touched and stroked with bare hands. *Martin Wegner*

So You Don't Want to Come Out?

Many cat owners are only too familiar with this sorry scene: a beloved cat is finally sweet-talked into the carrier, placed in the car, and brought to the vet. After a nerve-racking time in the waiting room, the carrier is placed on the examination table and the cat is now expected to confidently emerge to receive a shot. It's no wonder if, instead, he cowers in his safe cave and, with loud hissing and growling, indicates that he will certainly not come out voluntarily.

If you foresightedly bought a case that opens from the side, you and your vet can reach the patient without a problem and without lengthy coaxing. If, however, you are more traditionally minded and

find a wicker basket more romantic, you have a big problem—but more about that later.

You can train your cat at home, with the help of TTouch, to voluntarily leave the carrier. It's much better for the bond of trust between human and animal, to encourage the cat to leave the case under his own steam. You can achieve this goal by using a pastel colored straw, or a long, white riding whip (I call this the "wand," see p. 114 for order information) to stimulate the cat's sense of play and so gradually lure him out of his hiding place.

Your first playful outreach with the seductive "magic" wand, signals the cat that you intend no harm, and that in fact, you are offering him an interesting opportunity for "conversation." In some cases, a food treat can be helpful in luring him out of his fortress. Use every opportunity to leave behind a pleasant impression of the time spent together. Play and frolic with your cat for a long time and then try to gently TTouch him. When he realizes how pleasing these contacts are, he will emerge much faster from the carrier the next time. By the way, this training is good for more than just your next visit to the vet. When traveling, or attending a cat show, it makes it much easier if your feline isn't tuned to "stubborn!"

Case History
The Cat Camp

I am the director of "Kitty Camp," a facility that works intensively with cats that come from animal shelters. At "Kitty Camp," a

1. When a cat is especially anxious, it's best to make the first contact with a "wand" (a long, white riding whip) or a pastel colored straw through the door.

2. The door is opened in order to make direct contact.

3. Now I lift the top of the carrier and slip a soft towel into the space created between top and bottom.

4. I am doing light TTouches through the towel to give the cat confidence.

completely stress-free atmosphere prevails. I play quiet classical music around the clock and there are many trees and birds for the cats to observe when looking out of the windows. Sometimes, it takes a very long time for a cat to allow himself to be touched. Usually, I spend three weeks working on him with the wand until I can stroke him. I don't believe that my circling TTouches with the wand are always as precise as they should be, but they work. I believe that every kind of Tellington TTouch has a positive effect on cats. *Silvia*

Come Out of the Carrier!

Have you tried tirelessly to lure your cat out of the carrier using the wand, without the slightest success? The simplest solution would be to simply lift the cover off and let the cat come out in his own time. But this would spoil your chance at working with him.

If your cat is unwilling to come out because he is fearful or aggressive, open the case and raise the top, leaving a wide gap without unlocking the small entry door. After all, you don't want to unintentionally let your cat escape and hide under the living room couch for the next few hours. Now, slowly pull a towel through the opening from one side of the case to the other, so that he sits beneath a soft towel "roof." Under normal circumstances, you will need a second person to help you with this. One person lifts the cover

3

4

ABOVE: *I have gently wrapped the kitty in a towel and am performing little Circling TTouches on his head.*
BELOW: *At this point, the cat that was quite unsure, easily allows light Mouth TTouches.*

and holds the case steady, while the other pushes the towel between the two sections. Place the towel over the cat in such a way that he can't run away and yet can make himself comfortable under it. Your cat is still able to see out of the front of the case, which gives him a sense of security, but with the grid closed, there's no opportunity for him to escape.

At this point, speak softly to your cat, and begin making light TTouches through the cloth of the towel. First, try *Baby Chimp TTouches* on his back; it's easy to do and he will most likely not find it threatening. Continue with TTouches, even if he protests loudly or tries to evade you in other ways. You must give him the opportunity to feel the effect of the TTouches, and in a stressful situation it may take some time and patience.

TTouch has a calming effect. As soon as the situation becomes peaceful, gently wrap the cat in the towel and use one hand to hold it in place around his neck. Now you can work on the animal's face without being scratched or bitten. Do light *Ear TTouches* and *Chimp TTouches* on the head and around the muzzle, and stroke the whiskers.

Case History
A Cat Called Moose

Recently, I worked with Moose, a hissing, scratching, biting male, who seemed to be filled with both rage and fear at the same time. His leg had been amputated, but his basically negative attitude had apparently been a problem even prior to the operation.

First, I worked with all the usual tools that one uses in such situations: feathers, brush, a rubber hand—and I believe that these things had a positive effect on him. I also wrapped him in a

1. *I am using a cloth-wrapped "wand" to demonstrate contact pressures on the owner of a very fearful cat.*
2. *I initiate contact with the wand. The door is closed to offer the cat a sense of security.*
3. *Now, the door is open, and the owner and I speak to the cat in calming tones.*
4. *The decidedly timid cat now accepts being touched.*

towel, which I held closed behind his neck. This made him furious.

The next day, I simply covered him with the towel. He lay down and was actually quite content. Now, I could do light TTouches on him through the towel. The next day, I repeated the same procedure with the same success. If your cat also reacts with anxiety or anger when you wrap him in a towel, my advice is to simply place the towel over his body and work through it.

Moose's owners told me recently that he has become much friendlier and even allows people to pet him. I am still surprised at the amazing success that can be achieved with TTouch. *Rita*

The Wicker Basket

I have already mentioned that the traditional wicker basket is used for transporting cats as a beloved reminder of times gone by. Without a doubt, a wicker basket is much prettier to look at than a purely functional plastic carrier, however the latter can be thoroughly cleaned and disinfected, which unfortunately is not always the case with a natural product.

There's another problem: This type of carrier has a round, grilled opening at the front that is obviously meant for cats who happily walk in and out on their own. If your cat won't do this, you must reach in and pull him out. Clearly, you run the risk of being

bitten or scratched. In addition, sensitive cats feel extremely threatened when they find themselves cornered in a tight place and will often react aggressively.

If nevertheless, you are attached to the wicker basket, you should take some safety precautions for your own and your cat's sake. First, try working with a stick with a feather attached to the end, or the wand, to reach through the entry bars and make contact. If he hisses or strikes out furiously, don't get discouraged, but continue trying to arouse his interest in this new toy.

The next step consists of opening the grill door and making direct contact with the cat. For this, wrap the end of the wand in a soft cloth. If you're working with an aggressive cat, and there is a chance that you may be attacked, carry out this step with the grate closed. Make small TTouches with the wrapped wand, taking care not to do them too hard, or tickle the cat. In this way, there is a chance he will relax and calm down.

Claw Trimming

A cat's claws are the weapons that, in nature, he uses for defense or attack. Of course, a cat also uses them in other ways: A cat can hustle up the highest trees without a problem and walk easily on the narrowest of slippery surfaces. He can also use them to scratch itchy places that bother him to his heart's content!

A healthy, active cat wears his claws down himself and doesn't need our assistance. However, it's a different story with an older or ill animal. If his claws are not regularly and expertly clipped, they tend to splinter, tear, or grow so long that they turn downward, or begin to grow back into the sensitive paw pads where they can cause painful infections.

Claw trimming requires the utmost care. You should be sure to clip only the tip, otherwise you may cut into the part of the claw that contains nerves and causing a lot of pain. If you don't have experience trimming claws, it may be best to be on the safe side and leave the task to the vet.

Many cat owners have big problems with claw trimming.

Tip: For trimming claws you should use special clippers that you can buy in any good pet supply store or from your vet. Hold up the claw you want to clip against a light source, and you'll see exactly where the nerve runs.

Not every cat is eager to present his paws for a pedicure so you might do well to use TTouch as an aid. As long as your cat has not learned how to relax during the trimming procedure, it's helpful to have an assistant by your side to hold him. This way, both of your hands are free, and you can hold the paw in one hand while using the other to place the clippers at the right angle to trim the claw.

The procedure goes as follows: Rest the paw in one hand. With your other hand, make as many *Raccoon TTouches* as close together as possible all the way to the border of the claw. Then turn the paw over and work on the pads with light *Raccoon TTouches*. Follow this by carefully pressing your fingers into the space between the pads (but not so carefully that it tickles) and make tiny circles. Finish with gentle TTouches around the entire area

I am giving Puenktchen a sense of security by holding the sixteen-year-old domestic kitty against my body. I begin to TTouch one leg down to the paw.

Here is another way to hold a cat to stabilize the front paws. Puenktchen already has assumed a somewhat more relaxed attitude.

I work down the hind legs to the paws, using my thumb to make small Raccoon TTouches.

Here, I very carefully and gently, clip off the sharp tip of a long claw.

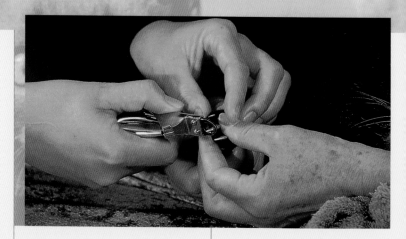

For claw trimming, it may be helpful to have an assistant.

of the claws. Tip: I find it useful to trim the sharp claws of kittens when they get to the stage where they are scratching everything in sight—our skin, unfortunately, included! One clipping session is usually enough.

Case History
Claw Trimming and
Fear of Being Picked Up
I have worked with TTouch on a regular basis for a while now, and am surprised by how well this technique functions and how successful the method has been for my seven cats. TTouch has been a great help in alleviating their fears, aggressive behavior and painful physical conditions. The most remarkable changes occurred with Breezy and Hazy Baby. While Hazy Baby still is

definitely aggressive, her former fear of claw trimming and being picked up has totally disappeared.

When Breezy was a little kitten she fell off our kitchen table and sprained her right hind leg. Although she recovered well from this injury, her leg remained sensitive and I was not sure she would accept TTouch. I worked with very gentle *Chimp* and *Raccoon TTouches* and she totally relaxed and expressed her pleasure with loud purring. In fact, she even turned over and offered me her other side for more TTouches.
Jolene Milsap-Rechagel

Sensitive Cats

1. My hand is supporting Heart's chest, which brings her into an upright position for TTouches on the belly. In this position, where the cat is held close to a person's body, the animal feels safe and secure.

2. Sitting upright against my body, Heart enjoys gentle Raccoon TTouches on her paws.

3. This young Burmese cat looks on a bit skeptically, as I TTouch her pads and talk to her calmly.

4. When I begin to do TTouches on the sensitive belly area, Heart lifts her leg.

5. I am testing the extent of Heart's trust in me, so I try gentle Tail TTouches. The cat is in no way disconcerted and seems utterly relaxed.

6. The beneficial effect of TTouch is truly manifested here. Heart lies on her back purring loudly and presents her belly to me.

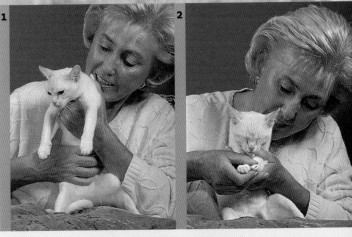

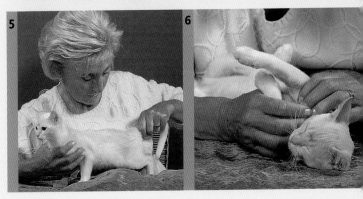

Circle *TTouches*

TTouch work for cats has been practiced for many years, and during that time I've seen seemingly magical results. Again and again, people send me reports of positive changes in their cats' health and behavior.

A New Method

Many people believe that once cats are adults, their behavior can no longer be changed, but TTouch has shown us otherwise. Even such deeply embedded reactions such as fear of the outdoors, shyness with strangers, or unwillingness to be held on a lap, can be changed. In addition, TTouch promotes general health, healing of the ill and injured, and deepens the relationship between human and cat. And that's not all. There are even more reasons to learn TTouch, as you will see below.

▶ **Family Cats**
The TTouch is helpful in many ways—for your cat, your family,

Circling TTouches are performed in connected lines over the entire head and body.

and you. Use the TTouch to accustom your cat to a new home after a move and to a change in the make-up of your family. You can calm down your pet when he's upset. You can show your children the way to have a harmonious relationship. Children who learn TTouch can develop a particularly deep partnership with the family cat. Through TTouch, they can learn to be attentive, friendly, goal-oriented, and patient. These characteristics are helpful in all other areas of life. I know a number of successful adults, who say that without the friendship of their cat, they would not have come through the difficulties of adolescence. I also know of cases where communication between parents and children was only made possible through common affection for their cat. And, should you have the good fortune to live with an elderly family member, you'll find that the cat is a wonderful nonverbal bridge between generations. Our four-footed friends do so much to enrich our lives—something we seldom stop to realize.

Animal-Shelter Cats

Some cats that have been brought to an animal shelter have no trouble at all being adopted, perhaps because they are so eager to be in a loving environment again. They come purring to the cage door and welcome each person who passes by. Such cats don't need TTouch in order to find someone to take them in and love them. There are, however, many domestic house cats that are also worthy of love but are shy or traumatized. They turn their backs or hide themselves in the farthest corner of their cages, trying to avoid attention. It's precisely in cases like these that TTouch is a lifesaver, turning a frightened animal into a wonderfully affectionate friend.

It's often impossible to make first contact with your hands. Give the cat time to gradually come closer. Wrap a soft washcloth around the firm end of the wand (p. 50), and use it to make the initial contact. Make gentle circles and light, stroking TTouches, and the cat will begin to feel more secure. To calm him, use body language and speak to him in soft, gentle tones. Sit sideways next to the cat, lower your gaze and turn your head slightly to the side. Blinking and licking your lips are also reassuring signals. I know of shelter cats that, after only three TTouch sessions of five or ten minutes, voluntarily came out of their cages.

I've also had a great many success stories with extremely difficult cats, who after TTouch, became as affectionate and responsive as you could possibly wish. It's important to be very careful and attentive with adult feral cats. I haven't known many, but among these were some who gazed at me with blazing, staring eyes, unmoving as a stone statue. They didn't react to gentle speech, reassuring signals, food, or repeated attempts to TTouch them with the wand. Such cats must be treated very carefully, because they can bite and scratch in an instant and escape with the speed of lightning!

Perhaps, at this point, you can't take in a cat yourself, but if you work on a shelter cat with TTouch, you can give him a chance he would otherwise not have of finding a new home. If you have already adopted a shelter cat, you know how traumatized they can be. For the first week after you bring your cat home, do five-minute TTouch sessions, and repeat throughout the day to help the cat feel comfortable and at home. Remember, with TTouch you are speaking to your feline friend through your hands, and you are creating a special bond and developing a close relationship with your new companion.

Being snugly held strengthens the feeling of security and self-confidence. Gentle, Baby Chimp TTouches do the same.

▶ Show Cats

TTouch is very helpful for "show-stars." You can use TTouch to reduce showtime stress before, during, and after the event: it takes only a few minutes of TTouch to prepare your cat for the trip, for evaluation by the judges, and for all the activity and noise in the exhibition hall. If you take the time to relax your star with TTouches at home, prior to the show, your cat will have a head start when it comes to the moment he is in front of the judge. I have had wonderful

This stunningly beautiful Maine Coon cat presses his head to my hand and enjoys the Clouded Leopard TTouch on his forehead.

results working with cats that were gorgeous to look at but who were so stressed by the whole event, they could not present themselves at their best. A few minutes of TTouch reduces not only the strain on your cat but your own stress, too.

Breeding

Cats have a variety of difficulties with mating, birthing, and the raising of their young. These problems arise more frequently with some breeds than with others. And, female cats who don't like to be touched or stroked are also more likely to have trouble with mating and are often unwilling to accept the male. If you count hyperactivity, oversensitivity, and nervousness

among the characteristics of your cat, TTouch is the remedy of choice. Before you even think about whether or not to breed her, take the time to change this behavior with TTouches.

To prepare your cat for the birth and for raising her young, do frequent, short sessions with the *Abalone TTouch* on the belly plus gentle *Belly Lifts*. These TTouches should only be used in the first half of the pregnancy to help relieve the cat of any discomfort. Very light (Number One to Two pressure) *Clouded Leopard* and *Raccoon TTouches* around the nipples will help prepare them for suckling.

Raccoon TTouches are a fascinating way to make contact with the unborn kittens. While doing these TTouches, imagine that you are creating a bond with the little ones. While you can maintain this same TTouch connection with the kittens after they are born, wait for a few days after the birth. It's important to leave the cat and kittens alone so they can get acquainted in peace. Early TTouching helps the kittens to grow up into calm, healthy, and socialized cats.

Therapy Cats

Cats that give service as therapy animals in hospitals and nursing homes can get very stressed. A cat will feel the emotional and physical suffering of humans and suffer right along with them. When a caregiver learns to use a light *Abalone TTouch* on her cat, it helps both the animal and the person. Just a five-minute session at the end of the day is enough to thank the cat for her effort.

Many cats need special training to work as therapy animals. When being held in the arms of a stranger, they must learn to remain completely unfazed by loud noises or sudden movements. Fortunately, cats seem to possess a particular awareness that permits them to easily adapt to the circumstances of nursing homes or a children's hospital. With TTouch, you can further the self-confidence and the special intelligence of the cats who work in these surroundings. For these specific situations, I recommend using all the TTouches.

Circle TTouches

Pressure Varies with cats on a scale from Number One to Three. A pressure of Three is the feeling of a very light pressure on your eyelid. Your fingers or hand don't slide on top of the fur, but actively push the skin.

Circle Direction Though Circle TTouches are mostly made in a clockwise direction, in some cases, a counterclockwise motion is necessary.

Tempo The speed for a one-and-a-quarter circle lies between one and three seconds. Nervous animals often need faster circles until they are able to feel comfortable with the basic circle speed of about two seconds. Faster circles are activating; slower ones are calming.

Pattern Circle TTouches should not be repeated in the same spot, but performed in rows a little distance apart and over the entire body. After a circle is complete, glide across the fur about a finger width to the next spot, and begin the next circle.

Names We have given the TTouches names that are easily remembered, which awaken an association, and connect to the animals I have worked with. For instance, the Clouded Leopard TTouch was inspired by a young leopardess I met in the Los Angeles Zoo. She had been weaned too young and had developed a neurotic kneading and suckling reflex. Small circles on her mouth and paws raised her awareness and the behavior stopped.

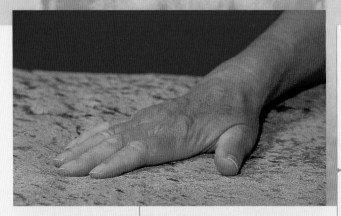

Above: *For the Abalone TTouch, place your flat hand on the body of the cat.*
Below: *When using the Abalone TTouch in small areas, your hand accommodates to the natural shape and curves.*

nervous animal will relax and calm down. This TTouch encourages a cat to breathe more deeply and release stress, even in a stimulating situation such as a cat show.

How To Place your hand very lightly on your cat's body. Imagine the dial of a clock: Begin at 6 o'clock (i.e. at the bottom), and with your palm, push the skin around once in a clockwise direction, continuing to 8 or 9 o'clock. Make sure that you move the skin with as little pressure as possible. You can achieve the best results by making the circles

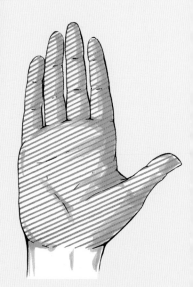

Abalone TTouch

Cats that are extremely resistant to being touched, very sensitive, or ill can profit from this TTouch. The warm, healing contact of the flattened hand provides comfort and security. If you pamper a cat with the *Abalone TTouch* and use this special way to deepen the human-animal bond, even a

slowly, taking about two seconds to make a one-and-a-quarter circle. When one circle is finished, pause and then slide across the fur a little way and make the next circle.

- **Case History**
Sassy is Hit by a Car
Yesterday, I brought Sassy home from the animal hospital. Considering that she was recently hit by a car, her condition is not too bad. The vet thinks there may be some permanent damage to her right eye. I don't know whether the eye can completely recover, but I've already seen that Sassy reacts excellently to *Ear TTouches* and very light *Raccoon TTouches*.

Sassy is actually quite shy about contact, however. If I hold her on my lap, relax her with *Ear TTouches* and comfort her whole body with *Abalone* and *Python TTouches*, she purrs happily. I am firmly convinced that the TTouch saved Sassy's life. Had I not known about it, I wouldn't have been able to help her. There were also positive changes in her behavior. Sassy had always been a shy cat—but today, I can pick her up and hold her without a problem.

These days too, she gets along beautifully with the other animals in my home. Sassy and my Boxer, Ariel, often lie on the bed snuggled close together. I think this is the result of my having done the TTouch on both animals during a single session, with Sassy on my lap and Ariel sitting on the floor at my feet. *Ginny Hawke*

I am stabilizing this quite unsure cat with my left hand on his chest, while using my right hand to apply gentle TTouches on his sensitive hindquarters.

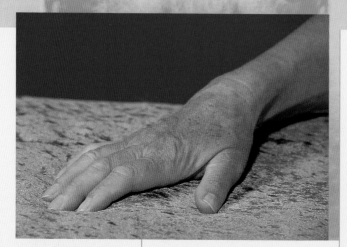

With the Lying Leopard TTouch, the hand is lightly curved, and the uppermost joints of the fingers move the skin around in a clockwise circle.

Uses

▸ **Relaxes tension**
▸ **Strengthens confidence**
▸ **Relieves fear and nervousness**
▸ **Calms hyperactivity**

Lying Leopard TTouch

With this TTouch, the warmth of the hand offers both relaxation and a sense of caring and security. This double balm is how the *Lying Leopard TTouch* is able to create a deep and lasting bond between you and your cat. Place your flattened hand on your cat's body, allowing him to feel its pleasant warmth. Then move your fingers with a gentle pressure.

How To Rest your flattened hand on your cat's body, then move the skin around with your fingers in a one-and-a-quarter circle. The shaded area illustrated here shows where your hand contacts the cat's fur. In contrast to the

Abalone, where you push the skin around with your palm, here you push the skin in a circle with your four slightly curved fingers. You'll be unable to place your palm on some parts of the body—the head and legs—because there isn't enough room, and because you can't keep your wrist in a straight position. When this is the case, move the skin around with the first two joints of your fingers, or, on very small surfaces, just with the first joint.

Your other hand rests, when possible, on the body of your cat, with your thumb, also lightly

resting on the fur, forming a connection to the other fingers. I believe that for cats, it's best to perform circles slowly and with a low pressure of from Number One to Number Three. Each gentle, one-and-a-quarter circle takes two seconds. When you finish a circle, pause for two seconds, and then glide a little way across the fur to make your next one.

This Maine Coon male, Earl of Devonshire, relishes the TTouch on his head.

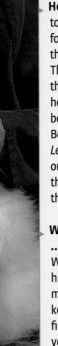

Head Most cats love gentle touches on the head and will rub it fondly against your hand to show they're in the mood to be stroked. There are, however, anxious cats that shy away from having their heads touched and must therefore be approached with great care. Begin with very gentle *Lying Leopard TTouches* on the forehead, on the side, and under the muzzle, then move to the neck and finally to the entire body.

What You Should Do if ...
... the Cat Won't Hold Still
Wrap your cat in a towel to keep him still, then concentrate on making your circles round and on keeping the pressure of your fingers gentle. Pay attention to your breathing, making sure to keep it even. Circle your hand in a

Gentle Lying Leopard TTouches build trust between cat and human. Here, Simalija, a Neva Masquarade cat, savors the contact.

Lying Leopard TTouches are pleasurable and heighten an animal's awareness of the body.

counter-clockwise direction. Interestingly enough, at the beginning of a session, some cats find this more pleasant and reassuring than a clockwise circle. As soon as the cat has quieted down, switch to clockwise circles.

Case History
Restless Nights

Before I learned the TTouch, Leo, my male cat, hardly let me sleep a wink at night. So, to help both of us get some rest, I began giving him TTouch sessions before bedtime. In the beginning, when he was still fidgety, I wrapped him in a towel and did two-second circles with a pause between each one. Though he now really likes these TTouch sessions, I still need to concentrate on quieting my own breathing. I have also added calming classical music to what has become our nightly ritual. Leo and I enjoy it very much, and he now allows me to have a peaceful night's sleep.
Anonymous

The fingers can also be spread apart a bit in order to stimulate the circulation.

Clouded Leopard TTouch

The *Clouded Leopard* is the basic TTouch underlying all the other Circling TTouches. It helps to renew your cat's well-being and to strengthen mutual trust between you. To make this TTouch, softly curve your fingers and work with a gentle pressure. The *Clouded Leopard* can be helpful in a number of different situations: For example, to calm your cat when in the vet's waiting room, or in the stressful environment of a cat show. Use it to center your cat's attention when he's nervous. The

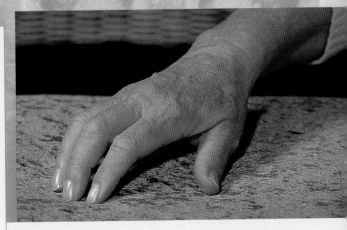

Clouded Leopard also helps to improve the coordination of cats with neurological disorders.

The circles of the Clouded Leopard TTouch are performed with the fingertips.

▶ **How To** Place your hand with the fingers lightly curved, on your cat's body. Then, using the pads of your fingers, push the skin around in a clockwise, one-and-a-quarter circle. For cats, I find it's best to place the fingers a little bit apart and allow each individual finger to make its own circle. The shaded areas of the fingers as shown in the drawing should be in contact with your cat's skin.

Your thumb rests with the lightest of contacts on your cat's body, thereby establishing a connection with your other fingers. However, with nervous cats, thumb contact is often not advisable. Keep your wrist as

Uses

▶ **Relieves stress, fear, and nervousness**
▶ **Strengthens confidence**
▶ **Introduces an unfamiliar evironment**
▶ **Increases body awareness**

Curve your fingers lightly and do the TTouch circles with an even pressure.

straight as comfortably possible so that your fingers, hand, arm, and shoulder are relaxed when you work. Place your other hand on your cat's body to lend support.

Start at 6 o'clock and push the skin around in a clockwise circle until you reach 6 o'clock again, then go on to 8 or 9 o'clock. The normal speed for completing one circle is one second, using a pressure of Number One to Three. When you finish a circle, pause briefly and then connect it to the next one by sliding along the fur a short distance. Picture a line between the circles and follow it. By doing so, you are connecting the TTouches to each other and encouraging awareness in your cat's body..

▸ **Whole Body Work** When you do *Clouded Leopard TTouches* all over your cat's body, you increase his self-awareness and enhance his feeling of well-being. Begin at the center of the head and do connected TTouches in a straight line across the neck, shoulders, and down along the flanks and back. Continue with similar connected TTouches in parallel lines when possible over the entire body.

▸ **Front and Back Legs**
Some cats don't like to be touched on the legs. If your cat is one of those, you can still try to carefully do the *Clouded Leopard,* even on this sensitive area. If the cat permits it, start on the upper part of the leg and move down to the paw. Try to space your circles evenly. You'll see tension release and anxiety dissolve, and notice a gain in your cat's confidence.

A cat may stand or lie down to receive these TTouches, whichever position is more comfortable.

▸ **Paws** The paws are an extremely sensitive area, and many cats don't willingly permit them to be handled. Nevertheless, try to execute the circles on the paws, using great finesse and a medium pressure. As soon as your cat realizes how pleasant the contact is, he will more than likely be glad to allow it. In addition, TTouch on your cat's paws will help him to become more grounded and surefooted.

What You Should Do If...
...the Cat Reacts Defensively
Cats have independent personalities, and can react to unusual situations with an inquisitive poke of the paw, a warning hiss, or a lightning- swift disappearing act. Therefore, don't expect your cat-friend to react to the TTouch with instant delight. Trust in the TTouch must be developed gradually, step-by-step. Sometimes, it might be necessary to contain a particularly obstreperous kitty in a large towel to prevent him from running away and to give him time to realize just how good the TTouch feels. If, however, as soon as you begin the TTouches, you encounter loud protests and strong resistance, it may be that you are using too heavy a pressure or that you are working on a hypersensitive area

of the cat's body. Slow your circles and work with different pressure strengths. If you notice that your fingers are stiff or that you are holding your breath, switch to another TTouch, for instance the *Chimp TTouch*.

If you want to give your cat's whole body a treat, it's best to begin at the center of the head and move down in increments until you reach the lower back.

▶ Case History
Duchesse—
The Animal-Shelter Cat
Duchesse was a stray that arrived at the animal shelter at the age of three. She had a friendly, but shy nature, and would withdraw as soon as someone approached her cage. Her stiff body and her wide-open eyes expressed her fear.

I approached her very slowly and worked on her with a variety

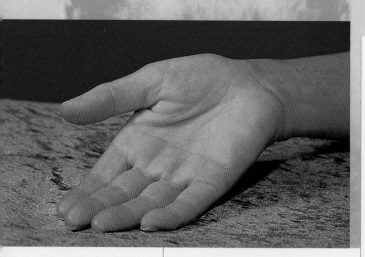

For the Llama TTouch, work with the back of your hand.

of TTouches for five to ten minutes. Although she was fearful, Duchesse did not try to bite or scratch me. The breakthrough came during our third TTouch session: The cat's eyes softened and she even pressed her head into my hands to be TTouched. When I arrived for our fifth session, Duchesse laid down on her side and stretched out her legs as I made small, gentle, *Clouded Leopard TTouches* on her body. Nothing proves the value of TTouch better than a success of this sort.
Bonnie Sanders

Llama TTouch

The TTouch is not always performed with the palm side of the hand. For cats that are sensitive and fearful, I use the back of the fingers, which they often perceive as far less threatening. It is for this reason that the *Llama TTouch* is particularly useful for gently accustoming a touch-sensitive cat to contact. Once a cat begins to trust you, you can then move on to other TTouches.

How To For the *Llama TTouch*, use only the back of your fingers to make the one-and-a-quarter circle. The contact should be very light. As

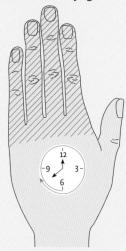

usual, begin the circle at 6 o'clock (with this starting point being closest to the floor), and push the skin around in a clockwise direction.

Head Anxious cats, when touched on the head, are apt to become stressed and even to tremble like a leaf. Place one hand gently on the cat's shoulder, and speak to him reassuringly while performing the *Llama TTouch* on his head with the other hand.

What You Should Do if...
...the Cat Doesn't Like to be Touched
For cats that are afraid of contact, the *Llama TTouch* functions as a perfect preparation for the other TTouches. The curved back of the hand is far less threatening to cats than an open hand, which they fear might grab them. In my experience, anxious cats will sooner or later accept these gentle touches made with the backs of the fingers.

Case History
Cats that are Difficult
Thanks to TTouch, I've experienced an amazing success with a supposedly difficult cat. I had been working on him for a long time with Bach Flower therapy and had observed a slow and positive improvement. Then, when I tried TTouch for the first time, I didn't think I had done a very good job because I had to stretch my arm under the couch in order to reach Tommy. However, the next day, Tommy came out from under the sofa all on his own and permitted himself to be touched while he ate. He still doesn't like to be picked up, but I believe he'll make good progress with this problem, too. *Sue Nill*

Uses U
▸ **Fear of being touched**

Even extremely insecure and anxious cats will often accept gentle touches done with the back of the hand.

For the Chimp TTouch, the fingers are loosely bent toward the palm.

TTouch allows you to touch your cat with precision and special sensitivity. Sensitive and touch-sensitive animals react positively to this TTouch. Cats that have had bad experiences with humans gain new trust faster because you are approaching them with the back of your hand rather than with the palm side. This makes it easier to touch cats who are extremely shy or who have been abused.

Chimp TTouch

Originally, this TTouch was developed for people whose hands are a bit stiff, inflexible, or weak. The name was inspired from watching chimpanzees and the characteristic way they use their hands when moving about.

The *Baby Chimp TTouch*, a variation of the *Chimp TTouch*, is particularly suitable for cats, and is performed with the backs of your fingers using the surface of your fingernails to the first joint. This technique enables you to touch your cat with finer, subtler movements than with the backs of the fingers between your first and second joints (the "large" *Chimp TTouch*). The *Baby Chimp*

How To Curl your fingers softly toward your palm, and touch your cat with the flat surface between

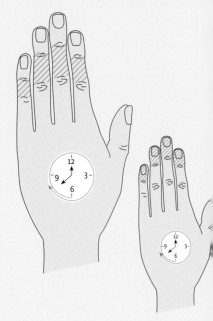

Uses

- Establishes first contact
- Builds confidence

The Chimp TTouch is suitable for making the first contact with a happy kitten.

the fingertips and first finger joint. Make the usual one-and-a-quarter circle. See the drawing for how to do the "large" *Chimp TTouch* using the backs of your fingers between the first and second joints.

Shoulders and Head A particular advantage of the *Baby Chimp TTouch* is that it enables you to use fine motor control to make gentle movements. Nervous cats are sensitive around the head and shoulders and need a delicate touch.

On the other hand, "normal" cats also enjoy the "large" *Chimp TTouch* on the head and face. Before working on your cat, try the *Chimp TTouch* on yourself, for

example, on your chest, using a Number One pressure and a slow speed of two seconds per circle.

Cats that have had bad experiences with people gain new confidence in humans.

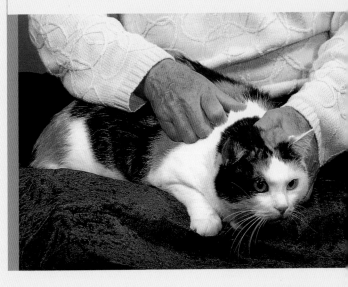

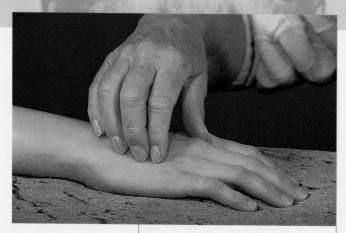

In the Raccoon TTouch, the fingers are bent at an approximately ninety degree angle to the body.

Raccoon TTouch

Old injuries or stiff joints can mean persistent pain for your cat. With the *Raccoon TTouch*, you can directly target sore areas and ease pain. If an area is sensitive, work as gently as you can to spare the cat additional discomfort. The *Raccoon TTouch* speeds healing processes and improves body awareness, especially in previously injured areas.

How To Bend the tips of your fingers at a sixty- to ninety-degree angle to the body, depending on the length of your fingernails. The circle is made with the tips of the fingers directly behind the fingernails.

Make an extremely small, one-and-a-quarter circle lasting one second with a pressure from

Number One to Two. If your cat is particularly sensitive, you may find he will better accept the TTouch if you don't use your thumb. To keep your TTouch light, the palm and heel of your hand should not contact the body. While one hand performs the TTouch, place the other on the body as a stabilizing contact. You can steady a nervous animal with the help of a towel or by placing one hand on the chest.

Tail The tail of a cat is a highly sensitive area. When working here with *Raccoon TTouches*, you should proceed carefully and with delicacy.

- Locates sensitive places on the body
- Treats injuries
- Accelerates healing processes
- Provides pain relief

With your left hand stabilizing the tail at the base, bring it into a position so that it forms a relatively straight extension of the spinal column. Then, using the thumb and index fingers of your right hand, work along the entire length of the tail with careful *Raccoon TTouches*. As you work down the tail, the left hand follows as a stabilizer. In this way, injuries to the tail, such as being caught in a door, will heal faster.

▶ **What You Should Do If ...**
...the Cat Won't Keep Still for TTouch on the Head
The simplest way to keep the cat still is to wrap him in a towel and enclose him between your legs, or else hold him encircled by your arm. If you discover any swelling or sore places, consult your vet;

the problem may be caused by a tooth that needs treatment.

▶ **Case History**
Booger's Infected Paw
Last summer, my outdoor cat, Booger, came home with a badly swollen and infected paw. I instantly took him to the vet who diagnosed necrosis and recommended immediate amputation of the paw. I asked him to bandage the paw, prescribe antibiotics, and give me the opportunity to work on the cat.

I made small, gentle TTouches all around the wound area, worked up the leg and finished by treating the entire body with TTouches. After three days, I took Booger to the vet again, and he could hardly believe the progress we had made. I continued the TTouches for a three-week period.

LEFT: *Raccoon Touches accelerate healing processes.*
RIGHT: *Sensitive and injured places are treated with the gentlest of Raccoon TTouches.*

Treat sensitive places with careful and extremely light Raccoon TTouches.

Today, Booger is a totally content, sixteen-year-old cat, and I am so glad that with the help of TTouch, I can give my animals a more peaceful and happy life. Thanks, Linda. *Kellie Brinton*

▶ **Case History**
Eye Problems
One night, I discovered a tear in the right eye of my nine-year-old male cat, Mercury. I examined the eye without finding anything obvious. The next day, I noticed that this eye was half closed. The vet examined the eye, discovered an ulcer on the cornea, and assumed that it had been hurt during a fight with another cat. He also found two missing front claws, which didn't concern him nearly as much as the eye. He thought that Mercury might have to lose it, and gave me antibiotics and eye drops.

Naturally, I did not, under any circumstances, want to touch the eyelid of the injured eye, therefore I did small *Raccoon TTouches* just above the eye. I followed this with extremely light *Raccoon TTouches* on the eyelid of the healthy eye. Mercury enjoyed the TTouches and even stretched his head out to me. To finish, I did small *Raccoon TTouches* on Mercury's front paws and also worked with TTouches over his entire body and ears. Each session lasted about five to ten minutes.

One week later, I brought Mercury to the vet again. He examined the eye and asked whether the injury was really only one week old. The wounds on the paws were also completely healed. The vet could not believe the speed of the healing process. When he acknowledged my success and asked me what I had done to achieve such results, I was truly convinced that TTouch can be a source of healing. *Terry Johnson*

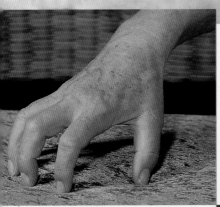

My fingers curve to resemble the paw of a tiger— but of course, they're much gentler.

ABOVE: *The Tiger TTouch is a useful TTouch for relaxed or confident cats.*
BELOW: *The Tiger TTouch calls for fast circles.*

Uses U

▸ **Establishes contact**

▸ **Promotes communication**

Tiger TTouch

This is a TTouch that we rarely use for cats. You can however, try it in the area just above the tail when your cat comes and rubs against you. Three or four short, light *Tiger TTouches* with the fingernails will do.

▸ **How To** Picture your hand as a tiger paw. Curve your fingers and hold them about a half-inch apart. Bend your fingers at the top joint to an angle of ninety degrees to the body. In this position, each individual finger then describes a fast, less than one second long, and continuous circle. The thumb maintains a light connection to the skin, without making a circle. You can rest your other hand on the body of the cat to stabilize her, however this is a matter of choice.

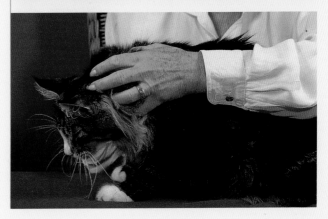

Stroking *TTouches*

Allow your hands to glide along your cat's fur with slow, stroking movements. The Lick of the Cow's Tongue, the Python TTouch, and other Stroking TTouches, stimulate circulation, calm down respiration, and enhance your cat's feeling of relaxation and well-being.

When doing *Stroking TTouches*, be careful not to make your movements too fast. Moving your hands too rapidly can awaken the cat's innate hunt-and-play instinct, or irritate and incite him to bite, thus hindering the relaxing purpose of these TTouches. Stroke over the cat's entire body, using a comfortable pressure and try to discover what rhythm he enjoys most. You know you've achieved your goal when your cat lies there purring, relaxed, and breathing quietly and regularly. If your cat reacts negatively to stroking, connect the circles for the first session and then change to stroking for the next one. Individual preference varies from animal to animal.

Noah's March

With horses and dogs, I often use *Noah's March* to initiate a session. Many cats enjoy a few light strokes on the head, neck and shoulders. Stroking over the whole body, however, is considered threatening by most cats because they are often extremely sensitive on the back and haunches. Therefore, use this TTouch if your cat is relaxed and you think he might enjoy it. It's good to use two to three lines of *Noah's March* to close a session and reintegrate all the areas of the body in which awareness has been awakened.

▸ **How To** Keep your hand relaxed and flexible so it can easily follow the contours of the body. Your loosely held fingers flow along the body with sensitivity and mindfulness. There is a clear difference between simply stroking and *Noah's March*. Through the long, attentive strokes of *Noah's March*, your cat gains an awareness of

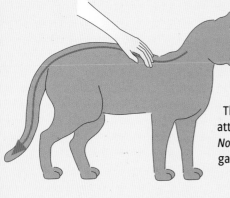

his body. He feels a sense of interconnected wholeness. Be really "present" with your cat and don't let your mind wander elsewhere. Feel the structure of his body under your hands—its warmth, softness, musculature, bones, and contours.

▸ **Case History**
Fear of Noise
We have two lovely cats, a Siamese, Robin, and a Shorthaired Persian, Tuck. One day, Tuck suddenly became frightened at the sound of the doorbell. Evidently, he associated the ringing with the arrival of strangers, so would run and hide for hours as soon as he heard the bell. Apparently, he didn't want to be seen or touched by anyone except us. Since both cats are regularly entered in cat shows, I did not want to allow Tuck's fear to build into real paranoia, so I took him to Sandra, who had been working with TTouch for a long time.

Sandra lured Tuck from his carrier, spoke to him reassuringly, and set him down on a table. Then, she showed me how to do *Lying Leopard TTouches*. At first, Tuck growled a little. His eyes narrowed into slits and his shoulder area

Uses

▸ **Calms through contact**
▸ **Completes bodywork TTouch session**

tensed up. However, after a few minutes, his body began to relax and Sandra was able to complete the first TTouch session with *Noah's March*.

I must admit that I remained skeptical, although Tuck had obviously totally enjoyed the TTouches. Perhaps the whole thing only worked in an unfamiliar environment, and when I tried it at home, the outcome would be different. Nevertheless, I was ready to try.

After the third TTouch session of five minutes, I noticed that Tuck was much more relaxed. I decided to put him to the test with a visit from my sister-in-law. She thought I was completely crazy when I asked her to remain outside the apartment and keep ringing the doorbell until I called to her to stop.

Tuck was lying stretched-out on the top of the dishwasher, and when my sister-in-law rang for the first time, he immediately sat up. When the bell sounded for the second time, he lay down again and peacefully busied himself with the job of cleaning his paws. Now, I work regularly with *Lying Leopard TTouches, Mouth TTouches, Noah's March*, and others. *Judy K. Churchill*

My hand performs calming strokes on the Norwegian Forest cat, Blue Bijou av Swalbod.

Noah's March is an integrating TTouch that connects all areas of the body.

One hand rests on the neck for stabilization, while the other glides further down along the back.

Some cats are particularly touch-sensitive in the area at the rear of the back. Be especially respectful here.

Some cats object if you glide your hand along the tail. Proceed with care here as well.

Python TTouch

The *Python TTouch* can be used on different places of the body, particularly on the legs. It is very effective when performed in combination with the *Lying Leopard* or *Abalone TTouches*. Using the *Python TTouch* on the legs, shoulders, or torso of your cat, increases circulation and general well-being. Stroking also has a positive affect on uncertainty and fear: Your cat gains mobility and balance. The *Python TTouch* can contribute to reducing anxiety and stress and can help to bring a new body image and self-confidence to an insecure cat.

Uses

- Stimulates the circulatory system
- Improves body awareness
- Strengthens self-confidence
- Relieves fear and tension
- Promotes balance and mobility
- Aids sensitivity to sound

▶ **How To** Place your flat hand on the body, gently push the skin upward, pause briefly, and then allow the skin to return back down. Make sure that your breathing remains even. If you use the *Python TTouch* on the legs, use your index finger and thumb to move the skin. For work on the upper leg, push the skin upward, pause briefly, and then return the skin back to the starting point. Then, gently slide a sixteenth inch

I am placing my flat hand around the upper portion of the hind leg and gently pushing the skin upward for several seconds.

Here, I repeat this movement on the mid-leg portion of the magnificent Neva Masquarade cat, Simalija...

... and end on the lower leg.

downward and begin the movement again. Push the skin as high as it will go without irritating the cat.

Combination (Coiled Python) TTouch

So, you've given a shelter cat the gift of a new home? It's likely that the time spent in the shelter left its mark on your new family member. The loss of the former owner and the atmosphere of the shelter can leave some cats disturbed, shy, and withdrawn. However, a multitude of other experiences can also lead a cat to a negative outlook on life. This is where the *Combination TTouch* can be helpful.

How To The *Combination* or *Coiled Python TTouch* joins a *Circling TTouch*—usually the *Lying Leopard* or the *Abalone TTouch*—with the *Python TTouch*. While the *Circling TTouch* awakens the animal's awareness, the ensuing *Python TTouch* deepens respiration and promotes beneficial relaxation. As soon as you complete a circle, let's

say, the *Lying Leopard TTouch*, with the flat hand at 9 o'clock, push the skin perpendicularly upward, pause, and bring it back down again.

Legs Since cats have slim legs, use your index finger and thumb rather than your whole hand to make the *Python TTouch*. For *Combination TTouches* along the leg, enclose the leg between thumb, index, and middle finger: Make a *Circling TTouch* with index and middle finger, ending with a *Python TTouch*. Enclose the leg beneath the elbow and after the first TTouch, slide downward on the leg a little to begin the next one. Continue in this manner until you reach the paw.

The *Combination TTouch* on the upper hind legs is done with your cat either standing or lying down. It's been my experience that this TTouch is most beneficial for cats who are stressed, lame, uncoordinated, or who are afraid of strangers. It is also helpful in preparing inexperienced show cats for handling by the judge, or for cats who are super-sensitive to noise.

Enclose the lower part of the hind leg with one hand. Make sure

Uses

- Improves body awareness
- Strengthens self-confidence
- Relieves fear and tension

The lifting motion of the Combination TTouch creates a sense of well-being.

that the position you choose is nice and comfortable for both you and your cat. When you have reached the paw, stroke the entire leg from top to bottom with *Noah's March*.

What You Should Do if...
...the Cat Refuses to be Touched
Either wrap him in a towel or use the "wand" as an extended arm to accustom him to contact. From a safe distance, sensitively stroke him with the wand, making small circles on the skin. Another method for using the wand is to wrap the tip in an Ace bandage and make the *Combination TTouches* with it. Some cats can also be convinced that this is a pleasant procedure by using a soft piece of sheepskin.

Case History:
Agatha—A Shy Cat
Ever since I began using TTouch with my thirteen-year-old cat, Agatha, she is no longer shy and reserved. Every evening now, she waits for me to give her a TTouch session, throwing herself completely into five or ten minutes of utter relaxation. Formerly, she was extremely difficult to handle, even more so with visitors.

Recently, I had to be away from home overnight and asked Martin to feed her. Before the TTouch work, though she knew him well, she would never allow him to touch her. This time, as soon as he came into the apartment, Agatha welcomed him and after she had eaten, signaled that he should pick her up. Martin bent down to her, stroked her and saw that she was extremely friendly. He then carefully picked her up and she was pleased to be in his arms. He was even allowed to stroke her belly. *Anne Snowball, TTEAM Practitioner*

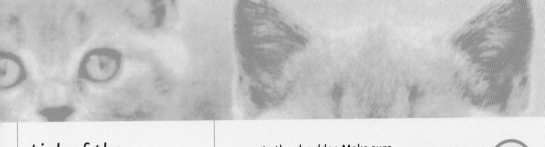

Lick of the Cow's Tongue

If you want to relax your cat while simultaneously stimulating circulation, give him a treat with the *Lick of the Cow's Tongue*. This long, sweeping TTouch, which is done with gentle strokes over the whole body, results in a definite increase in your cat's body awareness. In this TTouch, your hands gently stroke with or against the lay of the hair, whichever your cat finds most comfortable. Gliding over the body of your cat in different directional lines will increase his sense of well-being.

▸ **How To** Begin at the bottom of the spine and with fingers outspread, stroke against the lay of the fur up to the head. Many cats find this contact relaxing and enjoyable. The *Lick of the Cow's Tongue* improves body awareness and promotes the circulation in the musculature of the back. Next, glide your hand up over the back and across to the shoulder. Make sure to keep your fingers flexible so they can glide smoothly through the fur. To work on the back and belly area, begin the TTouch at the center of the belly and stroke across the flanks to the back.

▸ **What You Should Do if ...**
...The Cat Doesn't Want to Lie Down
Longhaired cats are often sensitive in the pelvic and back areas. Allow your cat to either stand or sit for this TTouch. Often, as soon as he notices that the *Lick of the Cow's Tongue* is enjoyable, he will lie down by himself. Breathe evenly and work lightly to create confidence. The relaxing effect of this TTouch is effective regardless of whether your cat sits or stands.

1. *I am doing long, Stroking TTouches to glide over the entire body of this stately Maine Coon cat.*
2. *I'm making sure that my fingers are flexible and my wrist is as straight as possible.*
3. *The cat is deeply relaxed, his eyes completely closed.*

Case History
Simon

Seven weeks ago, I took in a stray that had been hit by a car. He moved in small circles and dragged his hind leg behind him. His left eye was injured, and he had also suffered a severe head injury. The vet operated to remove the injured eye and two teeth. After four days, I took Simon home with me, however, he remained apathetic. He ate only when left to himself, and most of the time lay motionless on the bed. My neighbor, who had completed a TTouch seminar, began to pay us daily visits. She stimulated his depressed nervous system, and succeeded in awakening his interest in his environment. Simon began to run around and he even lay down on his side purring. Today, he has no problem eating with the other cats. Simon is very affectionate, self-confident, and has no problem running.
Cassandra Robertson

Tarantula TTouch

If your cat frequently reacts fearfully and does not like to be touched, try the *Tarantula TTouch*. This is light skin rolling, which activates the circulation of the cat. It reduces touch sensitivity and effects a lasting improvement in your cat's body awareness. Day by day, you'll see the trust between you and your cat increase. To experience the beneficial workings of the *Tarantula TTouch* for yourself, trade sessions with a friend.

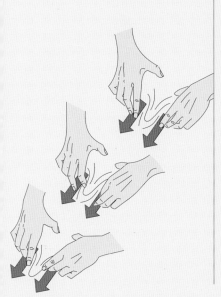

How To Place your hands side by side. The fingertips point in the direction you will be moving, while the thumbs are angled to the side and are almost touching. Now, both index fingers simultaneously take a "step" forward of about an inch with the two thumbs following behind like a plow. The skin in front of the thumbs is gently rolled by this movement. Next, both middle fingers move forward with the thumbs once again following behind. Index and middle fingers alternate with each "step," creating a flowing movement against the fur grain, leaving a visible track. Should your cat react uneasily to the contact on the back or the hind legs, start at the head and move as far as the cat allows while still remaining relaxed.

For the Tarantula TTouch, both hands move forward side by side, like two crawling spiders

Uses (U)

- Relieving touch sensitivity
- Activating circulation
- Sensitization
- Fear reduction
- Improving body awareness

Simalija likes the Tarantula TTouches on her back, which activate her circulation.

Tarantula TTouches are continued down the lower back.

▸ **What You Should Do if...**
...the Cat Reacts with Uncertainty

Begin at the head and carefully move toward the tail. Use the least possible pressure and slow down the movement. Many cats are particularly sensitive in the hindquarters. If the cat wants to run away and reacts with a twitching, lashing tail, or hissing, change to another body area or try a different TTouch.

▸ **Case History**
The Cat that Robbed His Owner of Sleep

A colleague of my husband, Alan, told him about her cat, who was in the habit of coming into the bedroom in the middle of the night, climbing up onto his owner's chest and falling asleep there. This was all right except the cat snored so loudly that his owner had to give up all thought of sleep. Alan showed the woman some TTouches and explained how to use them. After several days, she told him that although she had tried the TTouch only a few times, already her cat was bothering her a great deal less at night, and was also sleeping much more peacefully. *Nancy and Alan Smith*

both hands simultaneously toward each other, pushing the skin between them—pause briefly—and then return hands and skin to the starting position. Make sure to exert only as much pressure as you need to push the skin inward. The second movement that separates the hands once more is a relaxant and should therefore take twice as long as the first movement, which pushes them toward one another. Repeat these movements on various areas of the body. Do not forget to use your hands very gently, and time each breath to be in keeping with the movement.

Earthworm TTouch

This TTouch is helpful for cats that are sensitive and nervous, don't like to be picked up, or are afraid of strangers. It also serves to reduce stress in show cats during and after an exhibition, and can bring relief to cats who are plagued with stiffness and pain when moving. The *Earthworm TTouch* helps to ease and relax stressed areas of the body.

▸ **How To** Place both hands on your cat's back two to four inches apart. Gently and slowly move

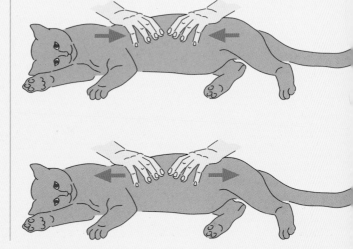

LEFT: *This Persian lady is pleased with gentle Hair Slides made through the fingers of the hand.*
RIGHT: *With longhaired cats, you can use both hands to slide along the neck fur.*

 Uses

▸ **Deepens trust**
▸ **Relieves grooming fears**
▸ **Relaxes**
▸ **Calms hyperactivity**

Hair Slides

Hair Slides are good for cats that resist brushing, are unwilling to sit on your lap, or suffer from neurological disturbances. Cats that refuse brushing are usually very sensitive or have, at one time, been brushed too firmly or quickly. I particularly recommend *Hair Slides* for longhaired cats, but it is also suitable for the shorthaired variety that dislike brushing.

Hair Slides deepen trust between you and your cat, and its relaxing effect is equally beneficial for both of you.

▸ **How To** Take a small bunch of hair gently between your thumb and index finger, or if you need to grasp a larger bunch, you can also use the spaces between the fingers of your flat hand: Now slide up the hair from the roots to the tips. This is done by going against the lay of the fur, grasping it gently between your fingers, and then sliding up the hair at approximately a ninety degree angle to the roots. A variation is to lift the hair gently with the fingers, pause, and then softly replace it again. Remain as close as possible to the roots of the hair.

This TTouch is very useful for activating circulation, reducing tension, and calming highstrung or hyperactive cats.

▸ **Head** Most cats enjoy slow, gentle *Hair Slides* on the head. This TTouch technique reduces nervousness and anxiety, and serves to reinforce the close relationship between you and your cat. For *Hair Slides* on the head of your cat, slide the hair with one hand and support the head with the other. *Hair Slides* are useful in many situations: at home, in the vet's waiting room, at a cat show, or during a long journey. In short, it is useful in any situation that your cat connects with stress and hubbub.

Hair Slides in the pelvic region prepare this sensitive area for brushing.

Shoulders and Back

Nervous and fearful cats mostly carry tension in the shoulder area. Allow your fingers to glide gently through the fur. *Hair Slides* are a perfect, gentle way to accustom a sensitive cat to the TTouch. When you work lovingly on your cat's back, he will develop better body awareness and more flexibility. For the back area, employ the whole hand—for small spots, use just the fingers.

What You Should Do if...
...the Cat's Fur is Too Short for Hair Slides

It's possible to do *Hair Slides* on shorthaired cats if you take a small bit of skin between your thumb and index finger. You can achieve tiny slides by first lifting the hair between your thumb and index finger, and then sliding upward along the hair with the thumb. When applying this TTouch, work from the head to the tail.

Case History
Henri—
Problems with Another Cat

From the time, two years ago, that we brought home a little stray kitten, our older cat, Henri, simply stopped being able to relax. He still gladly sat in my lap and even purred loudly, but then he would suddenly and without reason jump down and hiss, although no other cat was to be seen.

After I began to work on him with TTouches, Henri gradually returned to his old self and now he even follows me into the bathroom to be TTouched, without getting upset if the other cat comes along too. *Anonymous*

Specific TTouches

These Circle and Stroking TTouch methods are meant to directly target specific parts of the body. You can use them to calm your cat with TTouches on the ears, or to improve his mobility with legwork. Specific TTouches also speed healing.

Circling and *Stroking TTouches* can be targeted to very specific parts of the body. For instance, you can calm your cat by TTouching the ear, or improve his mobility with legwork. Working on individual parts of the body that have been injured also supports the healing process. In order to discover possible touch sensitivity and sensitive places on your cat, gently explore every inch of his skin. How your cat reacts may indicate either a systemic imbalance or an inborn characteristic. Figure out which is the case with your cat, and if in doubt, seek the advice of your vet.

The tail and the lower surface of the belly are generally sensitive areas, and some cats don't like being stroked or scratched on the back or hindquarters. With TTouches that are geared to particular parts of the body, you can work specifically on such sensitive problem areas while simultaneously preparing the cat for handling or medical treatment. For example, the *Mouth TTouch* is a good preparation for dental examinations, or the *Paw TTouch* for claw trimming. The *Ear TTouch*, *Belly Lift*, and *Tail TTouch* are usually helpful in preparing the cat to accept veterinary examinations more easily.

TTouches on specific parts of the body can also be used to ready

1 To begin the Ear TTouch, stroke from the center of the head toward one ear.
2 Slide further onto the ear and lightly stroke it. Then change to the other ear.
3 Stroke the ear sideways between thumb and forefinger. Imagine you are stroking a rose petal.

U Uses

▶ Calms and relieves pain

▶ Calms hyperactivity

▶ Stabilizes circulation

▶ Boosts the immune system

▶ Aids immediately after an accident

your cat for a show. For instance: the *Ear TTouch* can calm down your cat even in the midst of the most frenetic atmosphere. TTouches on the front and hind legs in combination with practice being held are good preparation for the judge's circle.

Ear TTouch

Most cats love these reassuring and soothing touches on their ears. Also, I've found the *Ear TTouch* to be the most effective way to calm a hyperactive cat. The *Ear TTouch* is a valuable first aid measure when you're on the way to the vet after an accident. If you immediately stroke the ears, you can sometimes prevent shock to the circulatory system. Applying the *Ear TTouch* as a support before and after surgery is helpful because it acts to stabilize circulation. Studies of acupuncture, a healing system that has been used for thousands of years, have shown that working on the ear can affect the entire body. TTouches on the ears can increase general well-being, balance the immune system, and support the nervous system so that it functions with maximum efficiency.

3

How To To stabilize the cat's head, sit with the cat facing away from you, and reach one hand from behind to hold him under the chin. To begin, use your thumb to gently stroke from the center of the head to the base of the ear, and all the way to the tip. Next, with the left hand supporting the cat's chin, the right hand gently grasps the right ear between the thumb and fingers in such a way that the thumb lies on top. Change hands to stroke the other ear. Work different areas of the ear so that every part is covered. Stroke the ears in an upward or sideways direction. The *Ear TTouch* takes a great deal of delicacy. Imagine you are stroking a tender rose petal. Slow, gentle stroking is calming and enhances the well-being of your cat—in fact, it can help to ensure a long, healthy, and happy life. Some cats prefer firmer strokes. If this is the case, work the ears sideways and use a firmer stroke at the base of the ear. To alleviate pain or shock, slide relatively quickly and more firmly along the ear.

What You Should Do if...
...the Cat Won't Let You Touch His Ears

If your cat won't let you touch his ears, make sure that he isn't suffering from an infection, ear mites, or other health problems. If your cat is healthy and yet still balks, hold his chin in your left hand, turn his head away from you, and with your fingers or thumb, bend the ear flap into the ear recess and make small circles, using a pressure that is agreeable to the cat. Next, make three or four firmer circles around the base of the ear and bend the ear into the ear recess. Follow this by stroking the ears downward and to the side between thumb and index finger. Cats that reject gentle stroking will often enjoy a different variation. This is also a good preparatory step before applying eardrops.

Case History
Caruso and Tango

Right after my three cats and I returned from a beautiful trip, I entered the worst period of my life. On Thursday afternoon, Caruso fought with the neighbor's cat. On Friday morning, I noticed that he was moving around with a bit of difficulty, and by Saturday morning, his entire hindquarters seemed to be crippled. I took him to the animal hospital, however no injuries showed up on the X rays. The vet's diagnosis was that Caruso had received a tiny, invisible injury, and he prescribed antibiotics.

I took my cat back home and worked with TTouches to improve his general health. A few days later, my other cat, F'lar, also showed unusual symptoms: spastic movements and strong salivation. I took him to the animal hospital, and the same vet who had treated Caruso earlier, diagnosed a virus infection and not poisoning, as I had feared. F'lar received an antibiotic and was allowed to go home.

That night, I was suddenly torn from a sound sleep by terrible caterwauling. I immediately thought my three cats were brawling with each other, but it turned out that F'lar was terribly agitated and seemed to be fighting with himself while the others looked on from a safe distance.

I picked up F'lar, and holding on to him with all my strength, I set him down on the sofa and began to work on him with *Ear TTouches*. My reactions were purely intuitive—I didn't even begin to think about what I should be doing. After about one minute, F'lar improved enough for me to take him to the hospital again. While driving there, I had to stop twice and do *Ear TTouches*, because the symptoms—although somewhat less—kept recurring. I realized that F'lar was suffering from seizures.

In the hospital, F'lar was examined and once again, we were sent home. On the following night, F'lar endured six large and several smaller seizures. I noticed that I could affect the length and intensity of the seizures with the TTouch. In the morning, we visited the vet, where F'lar had several more seizures. At home again, he continued to suffer seizures every thirteen to seventeen minutes until evening.

I worked on him with *Ear TTouches* over and over again, until finally, after two weeks, the seizures were under control. Next, numerous blood tests were taken, which showed that F'lar had contracted a virulent form of toxoplasmosis, which had affected his brain. The vet thought that two months of medicinal therapy would help.

At this point, Caruso was still crippled on one side, and it is only thanks to the work of a chiropractor that he is completely healed today. The miracle of F'lar's recovery was due to the fact that the TTouches gave me a certain amount of control over the seizures, enabling me to keep him alive until the medication finally became effective. Otherwise, his heart would surely not have withstood the numerous seizures. *Margaret Perry*

Case History
Joe—a Feral Cat

Joe was an amazingly beautiful cat with rich, dark fur. Somebody had caught the little feral cat in a trap, and then had splashed him with cold water to get him out of the trap and into a transport crate.

The day Joe came to me, he was already suffering with serious breathing problems. By the next morning, he lay at death's door. Thick, yellow mucus covered his

face, chest, and legs, and he lay on his side, hardly breathing. I took him to the vet who gave him several injections. After we were home again, I worked on him with TTouches every half hour for twenty-four hours. During the night, I believed Joe was going to die, but by morning his condition had improved and he even purred. Joe recovered completely and today is an extremely loveable and affectionate cat. *Helena Bresk*

ABOVE: *If the cat is unwilling to accept gentle stroking, try something else: press the ear against the head and slightly into the ear recess.*
BELOW: *Some cats prefer this rather firmer pressure on the ear.*

LEFT: *Gentle TTouches on the mouth stimulate the limbic system of this Norwegian Forest cat.* RIGHT: *The Mouth TTouch prepares your cat for dental and gum examinations.*

Uses

- Influences emotions
- Activates the limbic system
- Lessens stress, fear, and nervousness
- Calms hyperactivity
- Prepares for medication

Mouth TTouch

Joy, indifference, and aggression are governed—as are all other emotions—by the limbic system. The learning process is also activated by this highly sensitive region of the brain. When you touch your cat's mouth with intent, you can directly influence the limbic system and effectively moderate undesirable emotions such as fear, nervousness, stress, or hyperactivity. Many case histories demonstrate that it's possible to reduce aggression with TTouch. We have seen aggressive cats that enjoyed neighborhood territorial battles, react extremely positively to the *Mouth TTouch* and change their behavior in various ways. However, when the aggressive behavior is that of a mature,

unaltered male cat, then the chances of changing it are minimal, even if it stems from chronic pain like arthritis. When you use the *Mouth TTouch*, you are promoting the health of your cat's gums while also preparing him to more easily accept a vet's dental exam.

How To Start with L*ying Leopard TTouches* at the corner of the mouth, while using your other hand to support the cat's head. Next, move your hand along further forward on the mouth and do *Lying Leopard TTouches* to accustom your cat to gentle contact. End by stroking across the mouth, using both hands simultaneously, one on each side, and moving toward the back of the head.

In order to work inside the mouth, first hold your hand under

the cat's lower jaw and let your fingertips gently circle the outside of the upper lip. Then, slide your fingers under the lip and move across the gums with light, gentle circles—*Gum TTouch*. To allow access, simultaneously with the thumb of your other hand, carefully push the top lip upward. Repeat the same movements on the lower lips and gums.

What You Should Do if ...
...the Cat Won't Let You Touch His Mouth and Reacts Aggressively

Under no circumstances should you risk being bitten. Cat bites can be painful and dangerous. If your cat is repeatedly aggressive and shows his teeth, touch another part of his body to give him a sense of security. The *Mouth TTouch* may be more acceptable to the cat if you try using a warm, damp cue tip. If your cat is only slightly defensive, for example, turning his head aside, begin by using *Chimp TTouches*. With the fingers bent toward the palm, work circles in small rows, and try to activate the reflex that causes your cat to rub against your hand.

If your cat wants to bite, wrap him in a towel, stabilize him by holding it closed at the neck and use a sheepskin to do TTouches all around the mouth. Make sure that your cat doesn't have problems with his teeth or gums. If you remain patient, keeping in mind your ultimate goal, your cat will learn to enjoy the *Mouth TTouch*.

Case History
Chopin

Chopin is a former stray that we took in some years ago. One day, a fight broke out between Chopin and our other cat, Sabrina: it was the first sign of what was to become an ongoing problem. Chopin would ambush Sabrina and then attack her with teeth and claws. Twice, he even attacked her as she sat on my lap, and I, too, was

Earl of Devonshire delights in having his whiskers stroked. Stroke them backward simultaneously with both hands.

Left: *Suspicious and fearful cats gain security and confidence through Circling TTouches on the gums*
Right: *Use one finger to make light and gentle TTouches.*

You can use moistened cue tips for small or sensitive kittens.

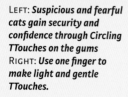

injured. All this happened before we learned the TTouch. I used to yell at Chopin, and chase him away. I knew that this was a useless thing to do, but I just couldn't think of anything else.

Then someone told to me about TTouch and I began to study the method. Chopin is a very affectionate cat, who enjoys being stroked, yet when TTouching him, I noticed that some parts of his body were very sensitive. At first, I had to hold him somewhat firmly in order to bring him into the correct position, with his head facing away from me.

He reacted particularly sensitively to TTouches on the mouth area, to *Abalone TTouches* on the back, and *Raccoon TTouches* on the tail. Today, we know that aggressive cats are often particularly sensitive in these regions of the body. I

worked on him daily for five-minute sessions until he finally no longer found the TTouches on the mouth and back unpleasant. A few days later, I was also able to do TTouches on his tail. The most amazing thing was that Chopin stopped attacking Sabrina. Though they didn't exactly become buddies, they are now able to live peacefully under the same roof.

Chopin was an excellent teacher, who showed us what a difference just a few minutes of daily TTouch can make, and taught us that TTouch work means more than mere stroking.
Debby Potts, TTEAM Instructor

Belly Lift

The *Belly Lift* is useful for cats who are sensitive, nervous, and hyperactive, or who suffer from digestive problems or the pain of illness or injury. It is also helpful in reducing stress, for example that of pregnancy or competition. *Belly Lifts* can be performed using either your hands or a towel.

How To *Belly Lift with a Towel:* the *Belly Lift* can be performed in various ways. You can use either your hands or a towel. Whichever method you use, remember to work as slowly as possible. When using a towel, gently lift the animals belly upward. Take three or four seconds to do so, and hold the lift for another three to four seconds. Then, while lowering the towel again, release

Uses

- ▸ **Reduces stress**
- ▸ **Relieves cramps**
- ▸ **Eases tension**
- ▸ **Relaxes the stomach muscles**
- ▸ **Deepens breathing**
- ▸ **Helps digestion problems**
- ▸ **Lessens back pain**
- ▸ **Prepares for pregnancy**

the upward pressure as slowly as possible. Lowering the towel while releasing the pressure is the most important element of the *Belly Lift* because it is the most effective. Start doing the *Belly Lift* first on the area right behind the elbows, then proceed toward the hindquarters by the width of your hand and do the movement once more.

Belly Lift with Your Hand: place your left hand under the abdomen of the cat, and rest your right hand on the animal's back. Then, with your

I use both hands to lightly lift the chest and belly of the Neva-Masquarade cat, Simalija, taking care that the cat's feet remain grounded.

Now, my hands release the hold to return Simalija's back to a relaxed position.

1. *You can also use a towel to apply the Belly Lift.*
2. *Slip the towel under and around the cat's belly.*
3. *The Norwegian Forest cat remains lying down and gets used to the towel*
4. *Now, I lightly lift the cat's body a little bit, something which he obviously enjoys.*

left hand, lift the belly upward toward the spine, but only with as much pressure as is comfortable for your cat. Hold this position for approximately three to four seconds, and then take as much time as possible to gradually release the pressure downward again. For first-time pregnancies, breeds known to have problems during pregnancy, or for mother cats who are not bonding with their young, I recommend adding small *Lying Leopard TTouches* to the lift, performed on the lower belly. Use this method only during the first half of the pregnancy. This *Combined Belly Lift* prepares the mother to nurse her young.

You can also perform the *Belly Lift* using both hands simultaneously, as shown in the accompanying photos. This is appropriate when a cat is secure enough not to need stabilizing with one hand. Lift both hands gently upward, hold the position for a time, and then very slowly release. Breathe calmly and evenly as you work.

TTouches down the foreleg encourage security, stability, and self-confidence.

It's a sure sign of trust when a cat permits you to make circular movements with her completely relaxed leg.

TTouch Circling on the Front Legs

Though cats are naturally among the animal kingdom's most skillful runners and climbing artists, they can still suffer from tension that may affect balance. Fear or nervousness, caused, for example, by severe thunderstorms or other loud noises, can often also affect balance. If a cat has neurological problems caused by an accident, TTouch on the forelegs can improve feeling and coordination. This TTouch is also useful as preparation for claw clipping.

How To You can do *Front Leg Circles* with your cat standing, sitting, or lying down. The movement is not forced, but takes place as the cat willingly releases his leg to you. Your aim is to awaken the trust that will allow your cat to relax and surrender himself totally to your hands. Each circular movement should be round, yet flexible, and should originate from the cat's shoulder. Be extremely careful not to stretch or put unnecessary pressure on the joints. One hand lends support under the elbow joint while the other moves the leg forward from the elbow. In this position, you can

Sensitive Python TTouches improve awareness in the foreleg.

Python TTouches can also be used on the lower leg — as here with Simalija.

Leg circles strengthen trust and ease acceptance

make the *Leg Circles* either perpendicular or parallel to the floor—in both cases, the elbow and wrist joints should be supported.

If your cat tries to pull his leg away, use no counter pressure, but wait until he relaxes the leg again and then try the circling movement once more. In our experience, it can be helpful to move the leg in the direction your cat is trying to pull it. You may also find that one leg can be moved more easily than the other. Such differences mostly are the result of chronic tension. Small circles are useful to release the shoulders.

What You Should Do if...
...the Cat Refuses to Relax his Leg

Many cats are not used to allowing their legs or paws to be touched. In order to make it easier for them, begin with *Circular TTouches* on the leg before you move on to the *Leg Circles*. Place one hand behind the elbow and initiate the leg movement from there, while the other hand determines the range and form of the circle. Determine also whether your cat is pulling away because his paws are ticklish. If that's the case, hold the leg on the joint above the paw and not on the paw itself. Ticklishness is reduced by TTouches on the paws.

Uses

- Improves emotional balance
- Releases tensions
- Stabilizes neglected cats
- Builds trust
- Prepares for claw trimming

TTouch Circling on the Hind Legs

Moving a cat's legs in circles relaxes the muscles, which in turn can lead to physical and emotional change and increased self-confidence. This method is a great help in preparing show cats for the judge's table. Circling and leg stretching help to relieve tension and nervousness. Small circles in all directions can improve coordination and balance for a cat that has been injured and must spend time recuperating. An added plus: Your cat learns to really relax and enjoy these movements. Cats also discover a new freedom in using their bodies.

How To Have your cat lie on his side in a relaxed position while you sit or kneel behind him. Support the animal's knee with one hand; with the other, lightly hold the leg above the paw. Now, carefully move the leg out from the hip and circle it in different directions. Carefully stretch the knee joint until the leg is nearly straight. Finally, bring the leg forward and move it back into its original position. Pay attention to making slow and fluid movements. Take only a few minutes and make sure that your cat is really enjoying it.

LEFT: *I stabilize Earl with one hand on his chest while I make small, Circling TTouches with the other.*
RIGHT: *Stretching the hind leg is a good way to build trust.*

What You Should Do if...
...the Cat Prefers to Stand Rather than Lie Down

In such a case, with the cat standing, support him with one hand on the rib cage, so he can keep his balance more easily. Then, lift one of his legs for just a short moment, and set it down again. As soon as the cat feels more secure, begin making gentle circling movements.

What You Should Do if...
...the Cat Favors One Leg

Leg Circles can substantially help to improve a cat's balance. After accidents, partial paralysis, and surgery, some cats will continue to favor one leg even though the healing process has long been completed. The memory of pain that remains stored in the cells can be dissipated by the use of TTouch. After the vet has determined that the leg is completely healed, make very careful and very small circles. You can also have the cat lie down to give him a sense of being grounded while you hold one hand under the paw and gently lift and circle the leg. Do the *Combination TTouch* as well, with a Number Two pressure, working down the lower leg all the way to the paw, and making sure to include the paw pads.

This Norwegian Forest Cat even stretches out his hind leg to provide me with better access to his inner thigh.

LEFT: *My arm gives Earl a sense of safety, while my hand works light TTouches on his forepaw.*
RIGHT: *This cat is observing the work on his feet with interest.*

Uses

▸ **Relieves fear of claw trimming**

▸ **Increases acceptance of contact on the paws**

▸ **Improves coordination after accidents**

▸ **Aids lameness**

TTouch on the Paws

As long as your cat is young and enterprising, you don't have to be concerned about his claws. Bold climbing adventures in the garden, or zestful claw sharpening on the scratching post, make certain that these razor sharp tools remain in good shape. With older, overweight, or downright lazy cats, however, it's essential to check claw length regularly, and equally essential for either you or the vet to trim them, otherwise they may grow so long that they catch on things. In extreme cases, claws that are too long can make it difficult to run, which in turn leads to stiffness in the shoulders and hips. Claws should also be checked to make sure they do not grow so long they turn downward and become ingrown. Since most cats

are extremely unwilling to permit claw trimming, it's a good idea to employ TTouch in plenty of time to prepare them for it.

▸ **How To** Your cat can sit, lie down, or stand up for this process. Before you start, relax him with a few of the TTouches he enjoys most. Then, starting at the top of the leg, do *Lying Leopard TTouches* down to his paw. Also, do gentle *Raccoon TTouches* on the paw, making sure to cover the whole area, if possible. The *Raccoon TTouch* uses only the fingertips. If your cat is ticklish between the paw pads, simply work with a bit more pressure. If the sensitivity is caused by long hair between the paw pads, cut the hair so you can have better access.

▸ **What You Should Do if...**
...the Cat Hisses
Does your cat hiss as soon as you

approach his paws? If so, use a bit of sheepskin to do connected, *Circling TTouches* down the leg. Stop every now and then to give your cat a treat so he will come to associate something pleasant with the procedure. If your cat is nervous about claw trimming, it's a good idea to have someone else hold him while you do the job.

**Case History
The Little Wild One**
My cat used to love to lie on my chest, but he'd then stretch out a paw, claws extended, and scratch my face. I began to make small *Circling TTouches* between his toes, and the change in behavior was immediate. I owe Linda a vote of thanks for showing me how to deal with his "careless" paws. Otherwise, I would have punished the cat and then perhaps he would have run away to scratch other faces. *Patrizia*

Tail TTouch

The *Tail TTouch* consists of small, gentle circles and light pulling. It is helpful for reducing fear and aggression, as well as increasing confidence in timid cats. This TTouch can also aid rehabilitation after an injury.

▶ **How To** The way a cat carries his tail is a part of his body language. An upright tail tells you that the cat is happy, while rapid tail-twitching is more likely to indicate that he is either in hunting mode or momentarily displeased. I've discovered that it's possible to have

Uses	Ⓤ
▶ **Decreases fear**
▶ **Reduces aggression**
▶ **Reduces insecurity**
▶ **Rehabilitates injuries**

When you begin the Tail TTouch, the cat may also be in a standing position.

This touch on the pelvis prepares the cat for the Tail TTouch.

I place one hand on the pelvis to offer stabilization, while the other strokes along the tail.

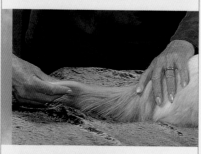

My fingertips very delicately smooth out the tip of the tail.

Do slow, gentle circling only when holding the tail at the base close to the body.

a positive effect on a cat's emotional reaction by applying the *Tail TTouch*.

The *Clouded Leopard TTouch* directly influences the nerve pathways in the tail. With these small and gentle circles at the base of the tail, you can make important improvements in the well-being of your cat.

To begin, support the body with one hand and with your other hand, gently grasp the base of the tail reaching from above. Next, stretch the tail out and move it in small vertical circles, rotating it in both directions.

Gentle "pulling" of the tail is also an effective TTouch. First, hold the tail at the base with one hand, create a gentle tension, pause for a moment, and then very slowly release the tension again. For this TTouch, the cat can either sit or lie down.

Do the *Tail TTouches* only in short sessions because your cat will have little patience for them. Cats are, after all, sensitive souls.

TTouch Plan for Your Cat

Name.............................. Age............................. Breed..
Use this chart to jot down your cat's reactions to the different TTouches.
For your notes, use a scale of 1 to 5: 1 = no acceptance, and 5 = optimal acceptance

DATE							
CIRCLING TTOUCHES							
Abalone TTouch							
Lying Leopard TTouch							
Clouded Leopard TTouch							
Llama TTouch							
Chimp TTouch							
Raccoon TTouch							
Tiger TTouch							
STROKING TTOUCHES							
Noah's March							
Python TTouch							
Combination TTouch							
Lick of the Cow's Tongue							
Tarantula TTouch							
Earthworm TTouch							
Hair Slides							
SPECIFIC TTOUCHES							
Ear TTouch							
Mouth TTouch							
Belly Lift							
TTouches on the Front Legs							
TTouches on the Back Legs							
TTouches on the Paws							
Tail TTouch							

Tellington TTouch Glossary

▸ **Abalone TTouch:** *Circling TTouches* with a perfectly flat hand; the skin is moved in a circle with the whole palm.

▸ **Belly Lift:** for relaxation. The cat sits or stands while his belly is gently lifted with the hands, or with a towel, held for a pause, and then very slowly released again.

▸ **Body Work:** a TTouch treatment session can also be termed *Body Work*. A normal session can last from just a few moments to ten minutes. When treating an injury, the time required may be longer.

▸ **Chimp TTouch:** a *Circling TTouch* done with the back surface of the fingers of the first and second joints.

▸ **Clockwise Direction:** the *Circling TTouch* is almost always performed clockwise, but in some cases, circling in the opposite direction can be more helpful.

▸ **Clouded Leopard TTouch:** the basic form of TTouch. It is a circular movement in which the fingertips and a softly curved hand push the skin around in a one-and-a-quarter circle.

▸ **Combination TTouch:** combination of *Clouded Leopard, Lying Leopard, Raccoon,* or *Abalone TTouch* with the *Python TTouch*. When the circle is completed, your flat hand then pushes the skin upward and slowly lowers it again.

▸ **Earthworm TTouch:** a very slow movement of both hands pushing the skin between them inward and then back out to the original position. It's best done on the cat's back.

▸ **Ear TTouch:** a *Stroking* or *Circling TTouch* on the ears. Stimulating the acupressure points on the ear has a positive effect on the whole body and can prevent shock from occurring.

▸ **Feather:** A feather is used to establish contact with cats that are anxious or sensitive.

▸ **Hair Slides:** evenly paced slides upward along a gathered bunch of fur— mostly done with longhaired cats. It relaxes the body and promotes circulation.

▸ **Leg TTouches:** a careful, slow stretch of the front legs moving forward from the elbow and back again. The same movement is used for the hind legs. This TTouch relaxes, increases awareness, and can improve coordination.

▸ **Lick of the Cow's Tongue:** long, diagonal TTouch strokes on the fur. The effect varies depending upon finger position. Softly curved fingers with the palm of the hand in contact activate; a flat hand calms.

▸ **Llama TTouch:** a *Circling TTouch* done with the back of the hand, which is less threatening to anxious cats than the open hand.

▸ **Lying Leopard TTouch:** a variation of the *Clouded Leopard TTouch*. The hand lies in a more flattened position; the fingers do circles as the palm produces warmth.

▸ **Mouth TTouch:** TTouches on and around the mouth and on the lips and the gums. *Mouth TTouches* activate the limbic system, which governs emotions.

Purring contentment! Two, happy new fans at the conclusion of their TTouch sessions.

Noah's March: a long, *Stroking TTouch* over the whole body used to introduce or end a TTouch treatment session.

Paw TTouch: small, *Circular TTouches* on the paws. It promotes "grounding" and helps overcome fear.

Pressure: varies with cats on a scale from Number One to Number Three. Number Three is measured as being equivalent to a very gentle, pleasant pressure on your eyelid. A heavier pressure of Number Four, or sometimes, even, Number Five, is used with dogs, horses, and humans, and very rarely, a pressure of Number Ten with horses and humans.

Python TTouch: a TTouch in which the skin is pushed upward, held for a pause, and then slowly released downward again.

Raccoon TTouch: a very light TTouch for sensitive places. The tips of the fingers perform small circles with the lightest pressure.

Tail TTouch: different movements performed on the tail—circles or pulling.This TTouch helps to relax sensitive cats and relieves tension in the body.

Tarantula TTouch: gentle rolling of the skin between thumbs and fingers in long rows, either with or against the fur line.

Tempo: the speed for a one-and-a-quarter circle lies between one and three seconds. Nervous animals often need faster circles until they are ready to enjoy the normal speed of about two seconds per circle. Fast circles are useful for their activating effect; slow ones for calming.

Tiger TTouch: a *Circling* TTouch performed with the nails of the fingers, which are held at a ninety degree angle to the skin and are curved and spread apart so that the hand resembles a tiger's paw.

TTEAM: acronym for the Tellington Touch Equine Awareness Method. Linda Tellington-Jones first developed this method for horses. Over the years, it was expanded to include many other animals and today is also known as the Tellington-Jones Every Animal Method.

TTouch: acronym for the Tellington TTouch Method, which includes the entire body of the work.

Wand: a long, riding whip (available from TTEAM, see p. 114). A child's fishing rod, or a feather duster can be used instead to gently touch or stroke the body of a nervous or aggressive cat.

TTouch Resources

USEFUL ADDRESSES

For further information about TTouch Training, TTEAM, Animal Ambassadors, Tellington TTouch Practitioners near you, Tellington TTouch Training Tools, or other publications by Linda Tellington-Jones, contact one of the following Tellington TTouch offices:

United States
TTEAM & TTouch Training Headquarters
Linda Tellington-Jones
P.O. Box 3793, Santa Fe, NM 87501
Tel: 1-800-854-TEAM (8326)
   1-505-455-2945 • Fax: 1-505-455-7233
e-mail: info@tteam-ttouch.com
web: www.tellingtonttouch.com

Australia
Andy Robertson
28 Calderwood Rd., Gaiston NSW 02159
Tel: 02-9653-3506
mail: ttouch@cia.com.au

South Africa
Eugenie Chopin
P.O. Box 729, Strathaven 2031
Tel: 27-11-8843156 • Fax: 27-11-7831515

United Kingdom
Sarah Fisher
South Hill House, Radford, Bath, Somerset BA3 1QQ
Tel: 01761 471 182 • Fax: 01761 472 982
e-mail: info@tteam.co.uk

Germany
Bibi Degn
Hassel 4, D-57589 Pracht
Tel: 02682-8886 • Fax: 02682-6683
e-mail: bibi@tteam.de • web: www.tteam.de

Canada
Robyn Hood
5435 Rochdell Rd., Vernon, BC   VIB 3E8
Tel: 1-800-255-2336
   1-250-545-2336 • Fax: 1-250-545-9116
e-mail: ttouch@shaw.ca • web: www.icefarm.com

Austria
Martin Lasser
Spitalgasse 7, A-2540 Vöslau/Gainfarn
Tel: 02252-700809
e-mail: TTeam.office@aon.at
web: www.tteamoffice.at

The Netherlands
Nelleke Deen
Ds. C. Spoorlaan, NL-72631 DA Nootdrop
Tel: 015-3699944
e-mail: nelleke@dest.demon.nl

Switzerland
c/o Bibi Degn
Hassel 4, D-57589 Pracht
Tel: 032-3853805 (CH) • Fax: 032-3853806 (CH)
e-mail: gilde@tteam-ttouch.ch
web: www.tteam.ch

Sweden
Christina Drangel
Svavelsovagen 11, 184 92 Rydbo
Saltsjobad
Tel & Fax: 08-540-27488
e-mail: jmpette@ibm.net

TELLINGTON TTOUCH TRAINING TOOLS

The TTouch Wand can be ordered from TTouch Training offices and online at www.tellingtonttouch.com.

NEWSLETTER

Keep up-to-date with all the news about TTEAM and the Tellington TTouch by subscribing to TTEAM Connections, a bimonthly, 24-page newsletter. It's dedicated to educating people about the TTEAM and TTouch methods along with other complementary ideas to help increase your understanding of animals and improve behavior, well-being, and performance. The newsletter includes: articles by Linda Tellington-Jones and Robyn Hood; case histories and letters from readers; and questions with answers from Linda and Robyn. Contributing writers include TTEAM and TTouch Practitioners and Instructors, as well as people from complementary fields.

TTOUCH TRAINING

Workshops

There are TTouch Training Practitioners through the world with over 150 in the United States and Canada, and 20 in England. If you would like to bring the magic of TTouch to your club or local cat group, you can host a two-day TTouch Workshop for companion animals in your area. All you need is a group of enthusiastic people and TTouch Training will send one of its highly qualified trainers to teach you and your group the proven benefits of using TTouch on cats. The workshop will cover the basic principles and techniques used in TTouch. Typically, you will learn how to:

- Learn the primary TTouches and when to apply them
- Deepen your relationship with your cat or dog
- Enhance the willingness and ability of your animal to learn
- Relieve symptoms of stress, such as lack of appetite or unfriendliness
- Help alleviate aggression and timidity in your cat
- Slow and ease the effects of aging

- Accelerate recovery from surgery or injury in conjunction with veterinary care
- Help your animals with common problems like unease and discomfort when traveling, aggression with other cats, manners, difficulty with veterinary visits, and many more

How to Become a Tellington TTouch Practitioner for Cats, Dogs, and Other Animal Companions

The certification program for TTouch Practitioner for cats, dogs, and other animal companions is designed for people who want to work with animals on a full or part-time basis and for people who just want to share the benefits of TTouch with their own animals. There are hundreds of professional TTouch Practitioners all over the world. Some work full-time with private clients, many do TTouch part-time in addition to their other jobs, and some incorporate what they have learned into their work with animals in shelters, obedience schools, veterinary clincs, and zoos. The rewards of this training program include an inspiring way to relate to animals, and for many, a new appreciation and understanding of ourselves and our own species.

The certification program to become a TTouch Practitioner takes approximately two years and requires a considerable investment of time and effort. The program is part-time and consists of six sessions (three per year) each lasting between five and seven days.

During the two-year, professional training and certification program, you will:

- Experience ways of working with cats, dogs, birds, and other pets that are unique, rewarding, and can change your life
- Acquire easy-to-use skills to deal with common behavior and health-related problems
- Use techniques to reduce stress in show cats

- Work with shelter animals to help them adapt more easily to new environments
- Learn how to help animals recover more quickly from surgery and injury
- Understand how TTouch inspires understanding and compassion for all life

For more information or to enroll in the TTouch Practitioner program, contact:

TTEAM and TTouch
P.O. Box 3793
Santa Fe, NM 87501-0793
Tel: 1-800-854-8326
Fax: 1-505-455-7233
e-mail: info@tteam-ttouch.com
web: www.tellingtonttouch.com

ALSO BY LINDA TELLINGTON-JONES

Books
Getting in TTouch: Understand and Influence Your Horse's Personality (published in the UK as *Getting in TTouch with Horses*)
Improve Your Horse's Well-Being: A Step-by-step Guide to TTouch and TTEAM Training
Let's Ride with Linda Tellington-Jones: Fun and TTeamwork with Your Horse or Pony
The Tellington-TTouch: A Breakthrough Technique to Train and Care for Your Favorite Animal
The Tellington-Jones Equine Awareness Method
Getting in TTouch with Your Dog: A Gentle Approach to Influencing Behavior, Health, and Performance

Videos
Tellington-Touch for Happier, Healthier Cats
Tellington-Touch for Happier, Healthier Dogs
The TTouch of Magic for Cats
The TTouch of Magic for Dogs
The TTouch of Magic for Horses
Unleash Your Dog's Potential: Getting in TTouch with Your Canine Friend
Haltering Your Foal
Handling Mares and Stallions
Learning Exercises Part 1
Learning Exercises Part 2
Riding with Awareness
Solving Riding Problems with TTEAM: From the Ground
Solving Riding Problems with TTEAM: From the Saddle
Starting a Young Horse
TTouch for Dressage

Acknowledgments

I wish to express my appreciation and thanks for the contribution of many friends and supporters.

To Gaby Metz for the delightful photos, charming textual interpretation of my work, and connections in the German show cat world that brought these lovely felines together for the photo shoot. To Gudrun Braun in her role as project director—thank you for your razor-sharp clarity, vision, creativity, support, and friendship. To Kirsten Henry for her innumerable suggestions and work on the original editing, as well as willingness to burn the midnight oil to meet the publishing deadline.

To Caroline Robbins and Martha Cook from my American publisher, Trafalgar Square, for your ongoing support, patience, and appreciation of my work. To Sybil Taylor, my treasured co-author on many other books, who for this manuscript acted in the important role of translator.

Thanks to illustrators Jeanne Kloepfer and Cornelia Koller for their excellent drawings.

A big thank you to Carol Lang in my Santa Fe office, and Gitta Maulshagen in the German TTEAM and TTouch office, for their help in seeking out the cat stories for the book; to Instructors Edie Jane Eaton and Debbie Potts for sharing their knowledge and experience with hundreds of eager students; and to all our Practitioners who are sharing TTouch with cats and their people. And, a very special thanks to all the breeders who brought their cats for the photo shoot: Dagmar Ertl-Hackstein and her Norwegian Forest cats; Ute Fehlhaber and her Sacred Birmas; Annegret Kesselring and her domestic cats; Andreas Marx and his domestic cat; Mrs. Mucher and her Somali; Christa Nuding and her domestic cats; Isolde Ollers and her Siberian and Neva Masquerade cats; Elvira Reibach and her Maine Coons; Gladys Salzberg and her Exotic Shorthair and Persian; Heidi Shultz and her Burmese; and Katherian van de Scheur and her domestic cats.

I would also like to thank Bibi Degn in Germany, Martin Lasser in Austria, Sarah Fisher in England, and Eugenie Chopin in South Africa for their dedication, leadership and organization of the certification trainings and TTEAM Guilds. And, to my sister Robyn's husband, Phil Pretty, my gratitude for his many contributions and support of her. I thank my husband, Roland Kleger, for his love, his positive critiques, his ability to provide just that missing word for an article, and for the joy he brings on our travels around the world.

Index

Page numbers in *italics*
indicate illustrations.

Abalone TTouch, 60, 61,
62–63, *62–63*, 112
Accidents, 63, 86. *See also*
Ear TTouch; Paw
TTouch
Adopted cats, 21, *21–23*,
23. *See also* Abalone
TTouch; Chimp
TTouch; Clouded
Leopard TTouch;
Raccoon TTouch
Aggression, 34, *34*. *See
also* Tail TTouch
Animal shelters. *See*
Shelter cats

Back of hand for
TTouches, *9*, *33*, *71*
Back pain. *See* Belly Lift;
Earthworm TTouch
Balance. *See* Hind Leg
Circles; Python TTouch
Behavior, affecting, *1–2*,
1–4
Belly Lift, 101–103,
101–103, 112
Body awareness. *See*
Clouded Leopard
TTouch; Combination
TTouch (Coiled
Python); Lick of the
Cow's Tongue; Python
TTouch; Tarantula
TTouch
Body language of cats,
33–35, *33–35*
Body Work (session), 112
Breathing. *See* Belly Lift
Breeding, 15, 60. *See also*
Abalone TTouch; Belly

Lift; Ear TTouch; Lying
Leopard TTouch;
Raccoon TTouch; Tail
TTouch
Bresk, Helena, 97
Brinton, Linda Kellie,
75–76
Brushing cats, 40–42,
40–42

Calming cats. *See* Ear
TTouch; Noah's March
Carriers for cats, 10,
46–50, *47–49*
Children and cats, 7–8.
See also Abalone
TTouch; Raccoon
TTouch
Chimp TTouch, *59*, 72–73,
72–73, 112
Churchill, Judy K., 80–81
Circle TTouches, 56–77
Abalone TTouch, 60,
61, 62–63, *62–63*, 112
Chimp TTouch, *59*,
72–73, *72–73*, 112
Clouded Leopard
TTouch, 60, *60*, 67–69,
67–70, 112
direction of circle, 61,
112
how to, *56–57*, 61
Llama TTouch, 70–71,
70–71, 112
Lying Leopard TTouch,
64–66, *64–66*, 112
pattern circle for, 61
Plan for, 111
Raccoon TTouch, 60,
74–76, *74–76*, 113
tempo of, 61, 113
Tiger TTouch, 77, *77*, 113
Circulation. *See* Ear
TTouch; Lick of the
Cow's Tongue; Python
TTouch; Tarantula

TTouch
Claw trimming, 37, 52–54,
52–54. *See also* Front
Leg Circles; Paw
TTouch; Raccoon
TTouch
Clouded Leopard TTouch,
60, *60*, 67–69, 67–70,
112
Coiled Python
(Combination TTouch),
83–84, *84*, 112
Combination TTouch
(Coiled Python),
83–84, *84*, 112
Communication. *See*
Tiger TTouch
Companion cats, *5*, 5–6.
See also Chimp
TTouch; Combination
TTouch (Coiled
Python); Ear TTouch;
Mouth TTouch; Tail
TTouch
Confidence. *See* Self-
confidence
Contact. *See* Chimp
TTouch; Starting
TTouch; Tiger TTouch
Coordination. *See* Hind
Leg Circles; Paw
TTouch
Cramp relief. *See* Belly
Lift

Defensive behavior of
cats, *35*, 79
Dental care, 27. *See also*
Gum TTouch; Mouth
TTouch
Digestion. *See* Belly Lift
Direction of circle, 61, 112

Ear care, 27. *See also* Ear
TTouch
Earthworm TTouch, 89,
89, 112

Ear TTouch, *94–95*,
94–97, *97*, 112
Emotional balance. *See*
Front Leg Circles;
Mouth TTouch
Eye problems, 76

Family cats, *6*, 6–7, 57–58
Fearful cats. *See* Abalone
TTouch; Clouded
Leopard TTouch;
Combination TTouch
(Coiled Python); Hind
Leg Circles; Lying
Leopard TTouch;
Mouth TTouch; Python
TTouch; Tail TTouch;
Tarantula TTouch
Feather for TTouches, *32*,
45–46, *45–47*, 112
Female cats, 15. *See also*
Breeding; Mother cats
Feral cats, 97
Foster cats, 23
Front Leg Circles,
104–105, *104–105*, 112

Gloves for TTouches,
42–43, *43*
"Golden Rule for Cats," 4
Goldfarb, Stan, 26
Good-bye (last), 29–31,
30. *See also* Abalone
TTouch
Grooming, 40–42, *40–42*.
See also Hair Slides
Guilt feelings, 31
Gum TTouch, 27, 100, *100*

Hair Slides, 27, 90–91,
90–91
Hawke, Ginny, 63
Healing, 2–3. *See also*
Raccoon TTouch
Health, *12*, 12–13. *See also*
All TTouches
Health Care Checklist, 27

Hind Leg Circles, 106–107, *106–107*, 112
Holding cats, 36–38, *37–39*
Hyperactivity. *See* Ear TTouch; Hair Slides; Lying Leopard TTouch; Mouth TTouch
Ill cats. *See* Abalone TTouch
Immune system. *See* Ear TTouch
Incontinent behavior, 15
Injury rehab. *See* Paw TTouch; Tail TTouch
Inoculations, 27. *See also* Chimp TTouch; Ear TTouch
Intelligence activated by TTouch, 4, *4*
Introduction to environments. *See* Clouded Leopard TTouch; Combination TTouch (Coiled Python); Ear TTouch; Hair Slides; Lying Leopard TTouch; Python TTouch
"Jekyll and Hyde," 3–4
Johnson, Terry, 76

Kittens, 9–11, *11, 17*, 17–18, 55, *55*. *See also* Abalone TTouch; Combination TTouch (Coiled Python); Ear TTouch; Hair Slides; Lying Leopard TTouch; Python TTouch; Raccoon TTouch; Tarantula TTouch

Lameness. *See* Paw TTouch
Leg TTouches, 112. *See*

also Front Leg Circles; Hind Leg Circles
Lick of the Cow's Tongue, 85–86, *85–86*
Limbic system. *See* Mouth TTouch
Llama TTouch, 70–71, *70–71*, 112
Lying Leopard TTouch, 64–66, *64–66*, 112

Males, unaltered ("studs"), 13–15, *14*. *See also* Breeding
Mastitis, 17–18
Medication preparation. *See* Mouth TTouch
Mobility. *See* Python TTouch
Mother cats, 16–18, *17*. *See also* Abalone TTouch; Ear TTouch
Mouth TTouch, 98–100, *98–100*, 112

Names for TTouches, 61
Neck tension. *See* Earthworm TTouch
Neglected cats. *See* Front Leg Circles
Nervous cats. *See* Clouded Leopard TTouch; Hind Leg Circles; Lying Leopard TTouch; Mouth TTouch
New cats, 11, *11*
Noah's March, 80–81, *80–81*, 113
Noise sensitivity, 80–81

Pain relief. *See* Ear TTouch; Raccoon TTouch
Parasites, 27. *See also* Hair Slides
Pattern circle, 61
Paw (infected), 75–76

Paw TTouch, *108*, 108–109, 113
Perry, Margaret, 96–97
Picking-up, fear of, 54
Plan for TTouches, 111
Potts, Debby, 100
Pregnancy. *See* Belly Lift
Pressure for TTouches, 7, 61, 113
Python TTouch, *82*, 82–83, 113

Raccoon TTouch, 60, 74–76, *74–76*, 113
Rechagell, Jolene M., 54
Relaxation. *See* Hair Slides; Lick of the Cow's Tongue
Resistant cats. *See* Abalone TTouch
Robertson, Cassandra, 86
Running away prevention, 35–38, *36–38*

Sanders, Bonnie, 69–70
Schmid, Oliver C., 23–26, *24–25*
Second cats, 91, 99–100
Seizures, 96–97
Self-confidence, 8–9, *9*, 21, 21–22. *See also* Chimp TTouch; Clouded Leopard TTouch; Combination TTouch (Coiled Python); Ear TTouch; Hair Slides; Llama TTouch; Lying Leopard TTouch; Python TTouch; Tail TTouch
Self-soiling, 27. *See also* Lying Leopard TTouch; Raccoon TTouch; Tail TTouch
Senior cats, 28–29, *29*.

See also Abalone TTouch; Ear TTouch
Sensitive cats, 55, *55*. *See also* Abalone TTouch; Raccoon TTouch; Tarantula TTouch
Session initiating or closing. *See* Noah's March
Sheepskin for TTouches, *14*, 39–40, *40*
Shelter cats, 21, 21–23, *23*, 58–59, 69–70. *See also* Abalone TTouch; Chimp TTouch; Clouded Leopard TTouch; Raccoon TTouch
Shoulder tension. *See* Earthworm TTouch
Show cats, *18*, 18–21, *20*, 38, 59–60. *See also* Ear TTouch; Hair Slides; Raccoon TTouch; Tarantula TTouch
Shy cats, 84
Sleep and cats, 66, 88
Smith, Nancy and Alan, 15, 88
Snowball, Anne, 21, 84
Sound sensitivity. *See* Python TTouch
Specific Body Part TTouches, 90–110
Belly Lift, 101–103, *101–103*, 112
Ear TTouch, *94–95*, 94–97, *97*, 112
Front Leg Circles, 104–105, *104–105*, 112
Gum TTouch, 100, *100*
Hind Leg Circles, 106–107, *106–107*, 112
how to, 93–94
Mouth TTouch,

98–100, *98–100*, 112
Paw TTouch, *108*,
108–109, 113
Plan for, 111
Tail TTouch, 109–110,
109–110, 113
Spraying (males), 13–14
Starting TTouch, 32–55
aggressive cats, 34, *34*
back of hand for, *9, 33,
71*
body language of cats,
33–35, *33–35*
carriers, 10, 46–50,
47–49
claw trimming, 37,
52–54, *52–54*
defensive behavior of
cats, *35*, 79
feather for, *32*, 45–46,
45–47, 112
gloves for, 42–43, *43*
grooming, 40–42,
40–42
holding cats, 36–38,
37–39
running away
prevention, 35–38,
36–38
sensitive cats, 55, *55*
sheepskin for, *14*,
39–40, *40*
strong cats, 44, *44–45*
towel-wrap hold, 23,
23, 36, 37, 38–39,
48–49, *48–49*, 50
wand for, 23, 47, *47–51*,
113
wicker basket carriers,
50–51, *50–51*
Stoklosa, Karen, 23
Stomach relaxation. *See*
Belly Lift
Stress. *See* Belly Lift;
Clouded Leopard
TTouch; Mouth TTouch
Stroking TTouches, 78–91

Combination TTouch
(Coiled Python),
83–84, *84*, 112
Earthworm TTouch,
89, *89*, 112
Hair Slides, 27, 90–91,
90–91
how to, 79
Lick of the Cow's
Tongue, 85–86, *85–86*
Noah's March, 80–81,
80–81, 113
Plan for, 111
Python TTouch, *82*,
82–83, 113
Tarantula TTouch,
87–88, *87–89*, 113
Strong cats, 44, *44–45*

Tail TTouch, 109–110,
109–110, 113
Tarantula TTouch, 87–88,
87–89, 113
Tellington Touch Every
Animal Method
(TTEAM), 113
Tellington TTouch for
cats, 1–31
adopted cats, *21*,
21–23, *23*
behavior, affecting,
1–2, *1–4*
Body Work (session),
112
companion cats, *5*, 5–6
family cats, 6, *6–7*,
57–58
"Golden Rule for Cats,"
4
good-bye (last), 29–31,
30
healing and, 2–3
health from, *12*, 12–13
intelligence activated
by, 4, *4*
kids and cats, 7–8
kittens, 9–11, *11, 17*,

17–18, 55, *55*
males, unaltered
("studs"), 13–15, *14*
mastitis, 17–18
method, 2–3, 57
mother cats, 16–18, *17*
names of TTouches, 61
pressure, 7, 61, 113
self-confidence from,
8–9, *9*, 21, *21–22*
senior cats, 28–29, *29*
shelter cats, *21*, 21–23,
23, 58–59, 69–70
show cats, *18*, 18–21,
20, 38, 59–60
therapy cats, 61
TTouch Plan, 111
veterinarians and,
23–28, *24–25*
well-being, *12*, 12–13
wellness of owners,
5–6
See also Circle
TTouches; Specific
Body Part TTouches;
Starting TTouch;
Stroking TTouches
Tempo of Circle TTouches,
61, 113
Tense cats. *See* Belly Lift;
Combination TTouch
(Coiled Python); Front
Leg Circles; Lying
Leopard TTouch;
Python TTouch
Therapy cats, 61
Tiger TTouch, *77, 77*, 113
Touch sensitivity. *See*
Llama TTouch;
Tarantula TTouch
Towel-wrap hold, 23, *23,
36, 37, 38–39*, 48–49,
48–49, 50
Travel, 10. *See also*
Combination TTouch
(Coiled Python); Ear
TTouch; Tarantula

TTouch
Trust. *See* Front Leg
Circles; Hair Slides;
Hind Leg Circles
TTEAM (Tellington Touch
Every Animal Method),
113
TTouches, 113. *See also*
Circle TTouches;
Specific Body Part
TTouches; Starting
TTouch; Stroking
TTouches; Tellington
TTouch for cats
TTouch Plan, 111

Veterinarians, 23–28,
24–25. *See also* Chimp
TTouch; Ear TTouch;
Noah's March
Videos and cats, *4, 4–5*

Wand for TTouches, 23,
47, 47–51, 113
Wegner, Martin, 46
Well-being, *12*, 12–13. *See
also* All TTouches
Wellness of owners, 5–6
Wicker basket carriers,
50–51, *50–51*
Worm cures, 27. *See also*
Gum TTouch; Mouth
TTouch